HAUNTED STIRLING

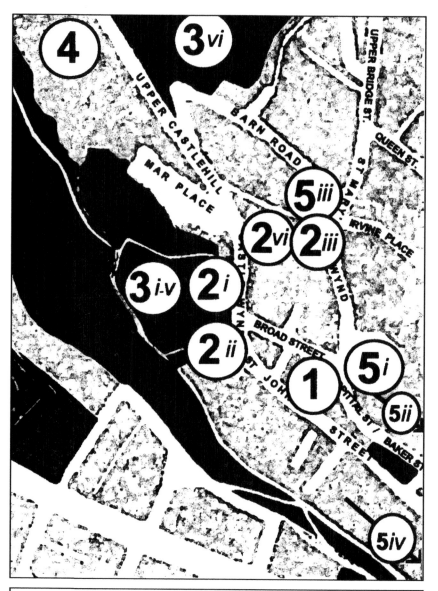

HAUNTED STIRLING

David Kinnaird

The
History
Press

For Eilidh Brown
(03.04.94 – 25.03.10)

First published 2010

The History Press
The Mill, Brimscombe Port
Stroud, Gloucestershire, GL5 2QG
www.thehistorypress.co.uk

Reprinted 2017

British Library Cataloguing in Publication Data.
A catalogue record for this book is available from the British Library.

ISBN 978 0 7524 5844 1
Typesetting and origination by The History Press
Printed in Great Britain

Contents

Acknowledgements

Thanks to Elspeth King, Michael McGinnes and The Smith Art Gallery & Museum (www.smithartgallery.demon.co.uk); Tony Murray (genealogy@stirling.co.uk); The Heritage Events Company/The Stirling GhostWalk (www.stirlingghostwalk.com); Brian Allan(www.p-e-g.co.uk/www.brianjallan-home.co.uk); the staff of the Tolbooth Theatre(www.stirling.gov.uk/tolbooth); Derek Green of The Ghost Club of Great Britain(www.ghostclub.org.uk); Willie McEwan, Ross Blevins and all at Stirling Castle (www.stirlingcastle.gov.uk); and Joyce Steel and the Museum of the Argyll and Sutherland Highlanders (www.argylls.co.uk/museum.htm).

Introduction

Their Pomps and Triumphs stand them in no stead;
Their Arches, Tombes, Pyramides high
And statues are but vanitie
They die, and yet would live in what is dead.
William Alexander, Earl of Stirling (Epitaph, 1640)

Do you believe in ghosts? It's a simple enough question, and one I've been asked many times over the past two decades as a performer and scriptwriter for the Stirling GhostWalk, a dramatic tour telling tales drawn from the rich heritage and folklore of the Royal Burgh, and performed before the glorious backdrop of the historic Old Town. Simple as it is, it's not a question which avails itself of a simple answer.

What is a ghost? Why do those whose days are done, whose bones lie buried in the dark and dusty earth, torment themselves in nightly visitation of those who live and breathe? Some say that ghosts are nothing more than shadows, memories, or moments of pain or passion trapped in time like a fly in amber. Others believe that spirits lack the will or wit to know that their days are done, and endure a breathless imitation of their former daily drudge, or that they are unable – or unwilling – to traverse the Crow Road that links our world with whatever it is that lies beyond. What binds them here? Unfinished business? An unrequited longing for love, honour or revenge? All of the above – if half the tales told of Stirling's Old Town have a word of truth to them.

My own interest in these stories has always lain in the quirks of their dramas, and their worth – whether they are true or false – in the cultural currency of the communities of the Castle Crag. Often the historical context of a tale, or the manner in which events manifest or are interpreted, can be as intriguing as the stories themselves. I've never seen a ghost. After two decades of living and working in a host of supposedly haunted houses, acquainting myself with the history and mythology of the area, I've yet to see, hear or feel anything that I could not explain – at least in part – by reasonable, rational, and utterly mundane means. I'm not even sure I believe in ghosts, at least not in the sense of a sentient, self-aware, persistent personal essence – but I'm open to the possibility. After all, if it is true that high emotions can somehow impress themselves upon a location, then it's no surprise that reports of hauntings have been so numerous in this town. From the blood and thunder of Civil War and the medieval struggle for independence, to the schism and strife of the General Strike; from the intrigues and infamies of the Stuart Court to the boisterous bustle of many a long ago demolished Broad Street slum, Stirling's turbulent, passionate past provides a rich resource of raw material – and a supporting cast which includes the likes of Wallace, Bruce, Burns and the ill-starred and ubiquitous Mary, Queen of Scots.

I have been fortunate that my work as a writer and actor has availed me regular access to the sites mentioned in the following pages, and has allowed me to participate – either as a performer or historical advisor (though I make claim only to being an enthusiast, not an expert) – in many studies of supposed hauntings in the town. I am grateful, too, that my status as a 'weel ken't face', if only in the ghoulish guise of Stirling's last hangman, Jock Rankine (of whom you will read more very shortly), has opened doors for me, helping persuade local people and genuine experts in the history of the area – Tony Murray and Elspeth King deserve particular mention – who have helped me root out the putative 'truth' behind some of the town's strangest tales. The Ghost Club's Derek Green and Brian Allan, of Strange Phenomena Investigations – both seasoned investigators with experience of a number of reputedly haunted sites in the town – have also been invaluable in their support.

This author, in my GhostWalk guise of Jock Rankine, the Stirling Staffman. (Image courtesy of Heritage Events Company)

Some of the stories which follow were well known to me – the Green, Black and Pink Ladies, and the murderous Alan Mair, have all frequently featured in GhostWalks over the years. Some tales, like those of Blind Alick Lyon, the 'Mar Changeling' and the 'White Lady of Rownam Avenue', are almost certainly apocryphal, but the manner of their creation speaks volumes about the nature (and endurance) of local myth. Others still – the strange twentieth-century tale of the 'Millhall Ghost', for example – were entirely new to me, and accounts of unexplained encounters in modern pubs and coffee houses bring us from the gothic gloom of the Old Town into the busy bustle of the contemporary city. I don't have an axe to grind, or anything to prove, and you'll see the sentiments of both the sceptic and the sensitive in coming chapters. As Hamlet said, 'There are more things in heaven and earth … than are dreamt of in your philosophy' – and, as an old schoolteacher of mine sagely warned, it is never a good idea to argue with a Great Dane.

I have focussed solely upon the stories of the Old Town and Castle Rock; Bannockburn and Breadalbane tales of the mystical Hand of St Fillan, Aberfoyle's 'Fairy Minister' Robert Kirk, and modern marvels such as the 'Cowie Poltergeist' will have to wait for another day. All of the sites mentioned, incidentally, are within easy walking distance of the modern town centre, and I hope that this guide will be of as much interest to heritage hounds as horror buffs. Readers with an interest in the history of the witchcraft and faery lore of the area can do no better than refer to Geoff Holder's excellent *The Guide to Mysterious Stirlingshire*. Those with more general tastes should seek out Craig Mair's *Stirling: The Royal Burgh*. Stirling's Smith Art Gallery & Museum on Dumbarton Road – just a few minutes' walk from the main Tourist Information Centre – is a wonderful place to acquaint yourself with some of the city's treasures first-hand.

Before we continue, a few words about Stirling itself. The etymology of the name – *Sruighlea* or *Stirlin* – is uncertain, but some suggest that it originates from an Old Scots or Gaelic term meaning 'place of battle' or 'place of strife', which would be fitting. A she-wolf rests, recumbent on our coat of arms, commemorating the fabled beast whose howls alerted seventh-century Northumbrian guards, then settled in their fortress of Urbs Giudi on the Castle Crag, to Viking invasion in dead of night.

A she-wolf watches protectively over the entrance to Stirling's Tolbooth. (David Kinnaird)

The dance of death – the seventeenth-century Sconce Lair. (David Kinnaird)

Some might say we have been howling at the moon, from that stern vantage point, ever since. It was one of the principal strongholds of Scottish monarchy from the time of David I, who granted Stirling status as a Royal Burgh in 1130, and was a favourite seat of the Royal House of Stuart – who took their name from Walter Stewart, Keeper of the Castle, High Steward of Scotland, husband to Marjorie Bruce (daughter of Robert I) and father to the first of that kingly line, Robert II. Next to the coursing flood of the River Forth, near the boundary between the Scottish Lowlands and Highlands, it was the 'Key to Scotland' – strategically important in every invasion and armed conflict to afflict the nation from the Roman stramash with Calgacus at Mons Graupius to the Jacobite Rising of 1745. Falling from courtly favour after the 1603 Union of Crowns, it became a hub of Caledonian commerce and light industry, with a busy port. It boasts a university, opened in 1967, and a population of around 45,000. Smaller than many of the country's larger towns, it became Scotland's newest city in 2002, as part of Queen Elizabeth II's Golden Jubilee celebrations.

On the subject of monarchs, where rulers have titles in Scotland and England – the norm after the Union of Crowns – Scotland gets 'top-billing' (this is a book about the 'Key to the Kingdon' after all). James the Sixth of Scotland and First of England will be rendered 'James VI (I)', and so forth.

David Kinnaird, 2010

one

THE TOLBOOTH

'Him That's Born Tae Be Hanged'll Ne'er Be Drowned' (Trad.)

The four faces of the Tolbooth's pavilioned Dutch clock-tower stand stern vigil over the Old Town and environs, dominating the Broad Street skyline just as the building itself once proudly presided over the judicial and commercial life of the Burgh. Where better than here to begin our tour of the town? Erected between 1703 and 1705 to the design of Sir William Bruce of Kinross, the 'Christopher Wren of North Britain' responsible for the remodelling of Edinburgh's Palace of Holyroodhouse, this stately structure's foundations date back to (at least) the twelfth century. Fines and taxes were paid here, and from the fifteenth century a council chamber and courtroom were added. In 1785 Gideon Gray extended the property. Gray also designed the Golden Lion Hotel in Stirling's King Street, then drolly designated as 'Quality Street' on account of the reprobates and roister-doisters residing within its drear tenements, taverns and coffee houses. One visiting villain, the 'ploughman poet', Robert Burns, was obliged to smash the hotel window upon which he had scratched his controversial 'Lines on Stirling' (*see* Chapter 4). Rabbie was fortunate that neither the sedition of his sentiment nor the vandalism which erased it from scrutiny was the cause of his own visit to the Tolbooth that same year. Though the 'ploughman poet' may have been discommoded by the Burgh's loutish local literati, he would have had much greater cause for complaint had he been forced to spend even a short time in what would soon be dolefully dubbed 'the worst jail in Britain'. Richard Crichton further extended the jail and courthouse in 1806.

Currently a theatre and arts centre, this imposing edifice has a suitably patchwork past, serving as a workhouse, and – in more recent memory – a restaurant, an artists' studio, a wartime army recruitment post, tourism development offices, and dressing rooms for public performances staged as part of the popular Royal Burgh of Stirling 'Living History' programmes of the early 1990s. It was in this last capacity that I first came to know (and explore) this fascinating building. My former dressing room, the Judges' Robing Room, is now the theatre bar.

For all its kudos as a contemporary cultural hub, the Tolbooth's history is as grim as its great grey walls. Geoff Holder gives extensive account, in *The Guide to Mysterious Stirlingshire*, of the many unfortunate biddies bound over, tortured and tried for witchcraft in earlier buildings to occupy this site, and a wall-plaque in Broad Street –

A plaque on the Tolbooth's Broad Street wall commemorates the hanging and beheading of John Baird and Andrew Hardie ('FOR THE CAUSE OF JUSTICE AND TRUTH') in 1820. (David Kinnaird)

formerly Market Street – commemorates the ritualised butchery, on 8 September 1820, of the weavers John Baird and Andrew Hardie. Commanders in the Radical War of 1820, Baird and Hardie were hanged and decapitated for High Treason after leading a protest march to the nearby Carron Ironworks 'FOR THE CAUSE', their plaque proclaims, 'OF JUSTICE AND TRUTH'. Dangerous men, indeed. It was not, after all, for the commoner to challenge his lot in life: a man – if his surviving letters, currently in the care of Stirling's Burgh Archive, are any indication – of passionate spirit and intelligence, Hardie's accusers saw in him as no 'martyr to the cause of truth and justice', as he described himself upon the scaffold, but merely one (according to a contemporary account of his unfortunate end) who was 'bred a weaver'. These dark deeds have all played their part in shaping the building's legacy. The Tolbooth, you see, has a reputation.

The Staffman

Thieves in the Burgh might find their hands pinned to the prison door on market day; perjurers their ears. Victims would be left to slowly and painfully pull their tattered, bloody flesh free, and those tempted to assist a friend in extricating themselves from such sorry situations might find *their* helping hands (or ears) hastily hammered by the town torturer, the Staffman (a title unique to Stirling).

The Executioner's cloak and axe, last used in the execution of Baird and Hardie. (Picture reproduced by kind permission of the Smith Art Gallery & Museum)

The last to occupy that onerous office was an unpleasant Ayrshireman named Jock Rankine, whose spirit – one of the Burgh's most enduring bogeymen – could once be heard each night in the alleyway adjoining the old prison. The tell-tale tap-tap-tapping of his ceremonial staff and his gasping, guttural growl echoed through the high-walled huddle of this mean vennel, the appropriately named Hangman's Close. The location of his official residence – 'a mere apology for a human habitation', according to William Drysdale's *Old Faces, Old Places and Old Stories of Stirling* – was a two-storey building with a crow-stepped gable to the street. The ground floor served as a stable, the first-floor residence was entered by an outside stair. A dingy close passed under the Staffman's house, connecting St John Street with Broad Street.

Torn down during extensive urban renewal programmes, which cleared away centuries of densely-packed lodgings and alleyways, Hangman's Close was supplanted by more modern (if considerably less durable) crow-stepped council housing in the 1950s. Many a local lad was warned to keep away from the wasted wynd when darkness fell, for fear that the Staffman would get them. To venture into its night-shrouded shadows was a test of many a Broad Street brat's mettle. This is oddly fitting, as in life Rankine's grumbling glower was infamous, making him a prime target for the constant taunts and tricks of the local 'kail runts'.

One of the perquisites of his post was the right to freely fill his Staffman's caup (cup), or 'Haddis-Cog' – the only part of the Staffman's official regalia to survive (displayed in the Smith Art Gallery & Museum) – from any merchant at the weekly Meal and Butter Markets, and fill his wooden Quaich at any tavern: privileges he greedily exercised at every opportunity. He served, too, as a sometime debt collector – on behalf of the minister of the parish. Jock's lack of good grace might have been better borne by the Burgh had he been more competent in the exercise of his duties. Drysdale recounts his less than sterling performance during the despatch of a young woman, condemned

The Staffman's house around 1860. (Image based on an original illustration by J.S. Fleming)

for throwing her illegitimate child from the Old Bridge into the River Forth. The execution involved the traditional Scots gib, a wooden beam fixed in a large stone, with a crossbar at its top, and a number of hooks fixed thereon. The condemned was made to ascend one ladder and the Staffman the other. After hooking and tying the noose, the executioner simply pushed the ladder away from the beam, and removed his own. Slow and painful strangulation followed. In this case, however, all did not go according to plan. The victim …

… had got hold of the ladder, and Jock was quite unable to perform his duty. Attending the sad scene were the town officers with their halberts, and one of them, Tom Bone, seeing the dilemma, went deliberately up, and gave the woman's fingers several knocks with his halbert, which caused her to let go, and Rankin succeeded in pushing her off. A good deal of sympathy was expressed for the woman, but Bone's vulgar and inhuman interference incurred the dire displeasure of the juvenile and female portion of the community, and he had to be escorted to a place of safety until the affair blew over.

For all the guard's cruelty, it was Jock's callous incompetence that was remembered. Legend has it that the 'last limb of the law' choked to death on a chicken bone strategically slipped into his soup by his surly spouse, a prostitute and sometime laundry thief named Isabella Kilconquahar, known to neighbours (on account of her impenetrable Irish brogue) as Tibbie Cawker. Under sentence in the dismal dungeon of the Tolbooth, Tibbie was offered immediate release – on condition that she married the Staffman and kept his house. She had cause to regret her choice of 'freedom'. Beaten and bullied by her new husband, no-one in the town batted an eye when she finally despatched the old gowk.

The Mercat Cross – viewed from the former entrance to Hangman's Close. Hangings occurred here between 1811 and 1843. (David Kinnaird)

His spectre's gagging growl is explained as his eternal effort to dislodge the fatal fowl-bone from his gullet. Too much dramatic irony to be true? Quite. This part of Jock's myth is pure invention – possibly created by parents eager to discourage their offspring, the descendants of the same errant *quots* who had plagued him in life, from playing in the derelict close – a night shelter for vagrants by the late nineteenth century. Stirling Town Council minutes for 2 February 1771 provide him with a more plausible (if less satisfying) end, revealing that the troublesome torturer was simply sacked for causing 'great annoyance and disturbance to the neighbourhood' and keeping a 'bad house', and provided with ten shillings sterling to get out of town. He died in Ayr around 1794. Current residents of the council houses built on the site report no continuance of the phantom Staffman's percussive presence, though he is still seen from time to time – as my own frequently favoured alter ego on the Stirling GhostWalk.

The Body in the Box

By 1842, when it was visited by Frederic Hill, Scotland's first reforming inspector of prisons, the Tolbooth was as feared and foul a destination as any felon might wish to avoid. As many as twenty prisoners – men, women, and children as young as six years of age – might be bundled together in each basement cell: unfed, unwashed and untended by their jailors. Muck and mire from the guttering running parallel with their tiny street-level windows would overflow into the cells when it rained, and it was said by one local physician, Dr Robert Forrest of Spittall Street, that 'more died there of the dirt than ever did by the hangman's hemp.' No surprise, then, that this place was declared by the prison inspector to be the very worst jail not just in Scotland, but in the whole of the British Isles.

In 2000, renovations by conservation architects Simpson & Brown were briefly interrupted when stonemasons made a most macabre – if not entirely unexpected – find. Beneath the recently excavated pend linking the original prison courtyard with Jail Wynd, the remains of a battered pine coffin were unearthed. Within were the crumbling bones of one of the most hated men in the Burgh's bloody history, a felon who was actually confined there at the time of Hill's visit, and who features prominently in ghostly accounts of the Tolbooth.

Alan Mair was a farmer from Candie End (Curshort), Muiravonside, eighty-four years old at the time of his residence within these walls. Any sympathy that Mair's maturity might engender would be woefully misplaced. He had shattered the skull of his sorry spouse, Mary Fletcher, viciously ending the poor woman's existence with his walking stick on 14 May 1842. A merciful release, perhaps, after the three decades of misery she had endured at her husband's hands. A pathetic creature, Mary was routinely starved or locked in a trunk for hours on end, as Alan dedicated his days to carnaptiously suing his neighbours over suspected slights or slanders. Her only relief came through the ministrations of outraged neighbours, such as Helen Bennie, who would release the wretched creature from her confinement each day to sup on

Alan Mair's coffined corpse was found beneath this pend during renovations in 2000. (David Kinnaird)

beef-tea – furtively keeping watch, lest Mair return unexpectedly and punish his wife for defiance of his will. Unsurprisingly, no doubt existed as to the old man's guilt when her death was discovered.

Mair was cast into the Condemned Cell, the uppermost chamber in the prison. The chain of his leg-shackles – still fixed firmly to the flagstone floor until the recent renovations – was just long enough to afford him a lonely view of Jail Wynd from his high window. It was perhaps hoped that this abominable octogenarian would demonstrate a sense of social responsibility befitting one of his great age, and have the good manners to simply drop dead and spare the Burgh the expense of hiring a hangman (by 1842 there was no longer a Staffman on the public payroll, and executions were rare). He had briefly entertained the idea of self-destruction, half-heartedly threatening a hunger strike, but as the anonymous author of one contemporary broadside put it, 'the cravings of nature became too much to withstand, and he afterwards partook of his victuals freely.' His healthy appetite provided further proof of his guilt for local gossips. In the months that followed, and despite the dreadful conditions of his incarceration, Mair clung to life like a miser to his last penny. He was unrepentant, scorning the comfort offered by Agnes, a daughter from his first marriage, and the counsel of the prison chaplain, the Revd Stark.

The Tolbooth – the Condemned Cell in which the murderous Alan Mair was held is upper right in this picture. (David Kinnaird)

Finally, on Wednesday, 4 October 1843, he was carried to the scaffold, bound to the stool upon which he had sat to enjoy his final breakfast. And here myth and history go their separate ways. According to local lore, Mair's wrists were bound behind his back, and a hood was pulled over his eyes. The noose was slipped about his neck and, just as he began one final scornful onslaught on the crowd, the executioner pulled the bolt. The trap opened beneath his feet. He dropped. The rope snapped tight about his withered gullet, and his feeble form jerked and twisted at the rope's end – but he did not die. Somehow he summoned up the strength to snap his bonds and, roaring with fury, his fretful fingers tore at the coarse hemp. The fearful townsfolk fell back, sure that the only way a man so old and frail could endure such a tortuous trial was through some diabolic intervention – that the Great Beast, Auld Hornie himself, had imbued the old sinner with the strength required to escape justice, and, no doubt, to wreak revenge upon those who came to mock him in his last moments of misery. Fearful that a riot would ensue, the executioner leapt from the gallows, grabbed the old man's ankles, and swung upon his legs until his efforts were rewarded and the murderer's neck was heard to snap.

That, anyway, is how *I* first heard the story of Master Mair during my first season as an actor on the Stirling GhostWalk, back in 1990. The truth of the matter is less melodramatic, but certainly no less gruesome. Alex F. Young's excellent *Encyclopaedia of Scottish Executions: 1750-1963* draws on contemporary accounts of Alan's appointment

Mair angrily protests his innocence in the 1991 Stirling GhostWalk. (Bonnie Nicolson)

with eternity. Tearful and trembling, the old man was carried to the gib, 'his whole appearance indicating the utmost degree of human frailty, borne down by the intense idea of grief.' He begged that he might be permitted to address the throng from the gallows. Expecting, no doubt, some plaintive plea for mercy from the old fellow, the crowd could hardly have expected the volley of vitriol which followed:

> The meenister o' the parish invented lies against me. Folks, yin an' a, mind I'm nae murderer. I ne'er committed murder, an' I say as a dyin' man who is about to pass into the presence of his Goad, I was condemned by the lees o' the minister, by the injustice o' the Sheriff and Fiscal, and perjury of the witnesses. I trust for their conduct that a' thae parties shall be overta'en by the vengeance of Goad, and sent intae everlasting damnation. I curse them with the curses in the Hunner and Ninth Psalm – 'Set thou a wicked man o'er them' – an' haud on thee, hangman, till I'm dune – 'An' let Satan stand at thyeir right haun. Let their days be few, let their children be faitherless, let their weans be continually vagabonds.

By this point in the murderer's surprisingly energetic oration, neither the crowd nor jobbing Glasgow hangman, John Murdoch, was of a mind to 'haud on'. The bolt was pulled, and in mid rant – 'I curse them a'…' – Mair dropped. He did free one hand – the other still being secured to the splintering stool upon which he sat. Then, as Drysdale reports, 'the hangman drew away the man's hand, pulled his legs, and amidst a guttural sound from his lips, and a yell from the excited crowd, [his] head fell to the side and he was dead.' There had been only a handful of executions in the Burgh in recent memory, and, for many, Mair's was the first they would have witnessed. And the last. As terrible as his crime was, the sickening sight of the old sinner's undignified end ensured that his was the final public execution to occur in the town. This was not, of course, Mair's only distinction: as far as I have been able to determine he was, at nearly eighty-five years, the oldest person to be hanged in Scotland in the nineteenth century.

Having alienated his only kin, his daughter Agnes, no-one claimed Mair's corpse. It was decided that his remains be boxed beneath the new step that was then being laid in the Tolbooth's Jail Wynd entrance, and it is here that Mair's spectral legacy is said to begin. For years odd occurrences were observed by those who knew the building well. Doors locked tight were found inexplicably open in the dead of night, and lights would come on unexpectedly. I firmly recall this happening frequently in the theatre space, formerly the courtroom, during rehearsals in the early 1990s. Older residents of the area spoke of gas taps suddenly hissing as valves opened without warning. In *Supernatural Scotland*, Roddy Martine tells of wine glasses toppling and door handles rattling during a reception marking the opening of the new theatre in 2000.

A decade earlier, in his monograph 'Alan Mair: Last Man to be Hanged in Stirling', local teacher and historian Craig Mair (no relation) reported an encounter with a waitress in Hermann's restaurant (now relocated in neighbouring Broad Street, and well worth a visit) which occupied the former cells at that time. The girl spoke of an uneasy sense of being watched by the spirit of an unpleasant old man, but only, oddly, on Wednesdays – the day, fittingly enough, on which the murderer had met his end. Another young woman, a receptionist elsewhere in the building, reported a curmudgeonly phantom furtively 'checking out' new female staff. Both avowed no knowledge of Mair. This in itself is curious, as most strange sensations within the building have been routinely put down to the malevolent old misogynist for decades.

It is important to note that, though rare, the old murderer's burial within the jail was not unprecedented. Other remains, including those suspected by some to be those of teenage poacher and murderer Alexander 'Scatters' Millar, executed in 1837 – who attempted to cheat a prophesy that he would 'die with his boots on' by kicking his shoes into the crowd from the gallows (a less than effective strategy, as his subsequent interment would seem to indicate) – were uncovered during renovations. Mair lay undisturbed until his grave was uncovered in 2000, and Church authorities were persuaded to allow him burial in an unmarked plot. The location of his new resting place is a closely guarded secret – lest revelation of its location offend those whose law-abiding kin rest nearby. One local rumour insists that the council, determined to ensure that the old reprobate was not tempted to resume his Tolbooth tricks, planted him under the watchful gaze of Alexander Meffen – first Chief Constable of Stirlingshire – at the foot of the Ladies' Hill.

'Poor John' and Other Encounters

Stage manager Rab Buchanan tells of a group of middle-aged women who visited the Tolbooth Theatre in 2007, claiming to have been drawn to the building by the spirits trapped there. They spoke of 'spectral vortices' and of ghostly children singing and dancing in the main auditorium, fascinated by all things bright and shiny. Happy, playful kiddies might seem odd in the former courtroom – certainly no-one else has commented on their presence – but their magpie tendencies might explain the still temperamental theatre lights. Children would have been resident within the building, at least during its brief use as a workhouse. These ladies were most vocal in their accounts of a malicious presence earnestly intent upon expelling them from the building. The energies of this entity (or entities) seemed focussed in the theatre entrance, the former pend where Mair's makeshift grave had been uncovered. Rab obligingly informed them of Alan's tale, but they seemed sure – rather surprisingly – that it was the shades of the martyred weavers, Baird and Hardie, who were eager to see them go. Curious, if true: although they were tried in the Tolbooth and executed in adjoining Broad Street, the radicals were detained (as traitors to the Crown) within Stirling Castle, spending very little time in the old jail itself.

Senior technician, Chris Waite, assisted me in a tour of the building in 2007, as I escorted a party of Edinburgh-based psychic mediums in a tour of supposedly haunted sites in the Old Town. All (save their driver – a sceptic like myself) were seemingly unaware of their destination, so Googling ghoulish details in advance of their visit was resolutely ruled out. We led them to the Tolbooth's stationery cupboard. Strip-lit, carpeted and shelved, it appears to be nothing more than a very modern store room. I gave the group time to collect their thoughts and seek contact with whatever wraiths or entities they believed were present. This done, I provided them with details of the site, drawn from documentary sources and the folk-record. Some of those present claimed that the site was 'too modern' or that the electrical lighting and air-conditioning were inhibiting their abilities. One pensive gentleman, though, commented that he sensed a great deal of anger in the room. Frustration, too. Someone, he said, had waited here – waited to die – and his seething fury was directed towards women. One in particular: a woman named 'Mary'. Interesting. Mair *did* wait an inordinately long time here – the former Condemned Cell, now radically refurbished – to meet his Maker, and his wife *was* called Mary. But while the purpose of the room in which we stood was not immediately evident, it was clear by this point in our tour that we were in a former prison, and Mary is an exceptionally common name. Proof of Mair's persistent personal essence? Certainly not. Intriguing? Oh yes.

In November 2008 I was called upon, again as an 'expert witness', to accompany another team of psychics whose impressions of the Tolbooth were being recorded for inclusion in a Fresh Film and TV Ltd pilot programme, *If Walls Could Speak*. Very few of their comments struck any familiar chords, being too vague to relate to specific historical accounts. With one exception – an encounter with a sorrowful spirit named 'John', a young man who had 'resisted death' and who still craved the comfort of his 'Faither'.

Moses looms over the courtroom entrance of Stirling's Tolbooth. (David Kinnaird)

The Tolbooth and Mercat Cross. (David Kinnaird)

One could not help but feel sorry for this poor soul, as the tearful medium told his tale. My initial thoughts were of John Baird – but he and Hardie, fuelled with earnest revolutionary zeal, had embraced martyrdom. John Smart (forger, 1788), hardly a young man at forty-nine, didn't fit the bill, nor did the feverish John Fleming (another forger, 1821), who seemed eager for his executioner to end his misery. John McGraddy, aged twenty-two (housebreaker, 1826), made two unsuccessful petitions seeking the clemency of Court and Crown, and was a possibility. Only as we departed into the chill of the night, the cameras long since packed away, did another possible candidate spring to mind – John Campbell, executed for housebreaking on 14 May 1824.

A feeble-minded teenager driven to distraction by knowledge of his impending end, Campbell's pitiable wailing from his cell – as the broadside issued on the day of his execution had it – 'arrested and annoyed the passengers on the streets' in the days preceding his hanging. Taken to the gallows, he struggled in vain to seize the rope and free himself as he was 'thrown off', all the while begging that his father forgive him for his wicked ways. Campbell had been one of the few felons to escape from the prison (albeit briefly). His father had shared his heir's desperate desire to cling to this mortal coil – employing a St Ninians physician to attempt reanimation of the corpse by means of blood-letting. He failed. Again, the supposed psychic's comments were vague, but Campbell's obscure case certainly seems to hit a few of the right biographical buttons.

This was not, of course, the first filmed investigation of the old jail. In early March 1992, a team from Strange Phenomena Investigations (SPI) was invited to the Tolbooth

Market Street in the early nineteenth century – Mair, Campbell, Baird, Hardie and many others met their end in the shadow of the Tolbooth. (Picture reproduced by kind permission of the Smith Art Gallery & Museum)

as part of a feature for the US paranormal television programme, *Sightings*. During their visit, mediums attempted the 'Spirit Rescue' of one of the Tolbooth's trapped and troubled souls. In the Condemned Cell (confusingly referred to in the programme as being *within* the castle), one psychic, Rose-Mairi Tognin, appeared to become temporarily possessed by a male spirit – anxiously exclaiming, 'They're attacking me! They're bringing me back!' – while another, Ian Shanes, sought to release the revenant from its new physical host. The mediums believed that they were able to relieve the spirit's suffering. 'I felt it escape,' said Tognin, afterwards. 'I felt it physically and I felt it emotionally. The pressure began to just evaporate from me.' Shanes concurred; 'He wanted out, and he got an out. He got that door that he wanted.' Which of the jail's ghosts was reputedly rescued is unclear. The late Cambridge investigator Tony Cornell, part of another team working in Stirling for the programme, was more cautiously sceptical of this encounter, warily describing the psychics' findings as 'too melodramatic. Sincere, but I don't think it was correct.' If a rescue was affected then the spirit was fortunate, as escapes from the Tolbooth were rare.

Rab, Chris, myself, and another Technician, James Wigglesworth, have all had cause over the years to spend nights alone in the Tolbooth, and can testify to the typically spooky creaks and bumps that old buildings bring with them. Knowing the site's history, it is all too easy to imbue some dark and dismal significance onto the most mundane happenstance. None of us, though, have ever been particularly upset or unsettled by the place, possibly because we are acclimatised to the noisily nocturnal settling of timbers and the wheeze and groan of ancient air flues. James, however, confesses to one odd experience. Entering the building in the dead of night, some years ago, inspired to complete some personal project or other, he heard a short, sharp bang in the distant darkness of the stairwell. With a cry of, 'Okay. You win!' he turned on his heels and decided on a not-*quite*-so-early start, instead – freed from the prospective perils of his own imaginings – he returned in the comforting light of the new dawn.

An interesting epilogue. *The Guide to Mysterious Stirlingshire* reports the 2002 experience of a local postman, startled by the sudden appearance of a ghoulish figure garbed in nineteenth-century clothing in the theatre's Jail Wynd pend. The figure offered a breathy 'Good mornin' to you!' – far too gregarious a greeting for the grumpy Mr Mair who was, as Geoff Holder puts it, 'more of a snarl than a greeting kind of chap'. Quite so. *I*, on the other hand, am far friendlier (most of the time). It was yours-truly, garbed in the attire of prison inspector Frederic Hill, who alarmed the petrified postie as I hot-footed from the Darnley Coffee House, BLT in hand, up Broad Street and through the Wynd to an impending performance at the neighbouring Stirling Old Town Jail.

The Old Town Jail provides another link to 'Auld Alan' – albeit a most unexpected and unwelcome one. Built by reformers to replace the Tolbooth, this building served as the Burgh prison from 1847 until 1888, and as Scotland's military Detention Barracks until the mid-1930s, after which time it fell rapidly into decline. Many older locals know it as 'The Sweetie Factory', from its time as a storage facility for the Caledonian Confectionery Co. Redeveloped as office space and a modern visitor attraction, it

Old Town Jail – the reformed prison which replaced the terrible Tolbooth. (David Kinnaird)

opened its doors to the public in Easter 1996. As renovations concluded, rehearsals for actor-led jail tours began. During one session, directing another performer, I somehow managed to damage the ligament in my leg and had to be carried out of the building, strapped to a chair. Amused by the memory that Mair had to be carried out of *his* prison in just this way, I decided then and there to include his tale in that year's GhostWalk, though one superstitious colleague complained that I was 'tempting fate' – 'Auld Alan' would not be amused. Months later, my musculature on the mend, I leapt out on my first audience of the summer season garbed as the grim old ghoul – and felt the damaged ligament strain and snap beneath me. Unable to support myself on the steep slope of King's Stables Lane, and with only a few minutes left until the tour's end, I elected to hold true to the time-honoured theatrical idiom that 'the show must go on' and persuaded members of my audience to carry me to the finale in Cowane's House – a re-enactment of the wife-beater's execution, to which he was yet again being carried by a jeering mob. Bad luck, or the fiendish farmer's wrath? Either way, no-one likes a critic.

two

Famous Sons

'Better A Guid Name Than A Fine Face' (Trad.)

The Curse of Alloa Tower

Mar's Wark, Mar Place

In October 2009, following a performance of the Stirling Ghost Walk, I was approached by an audience member – Barbara, from Menstrie – who had become increasingly agitated during the show's last few moments. Concerned that my storytelling might have inadvertently upset her (a dent to any actor's ego), I was reassured to find that I was not the cause of her distress. As I launched into my final monologue she had become aware, she said, of the cry of a child – a baby – echoing within the walls of the surrounding ruin. This staid and sensible matron was surprised that no-one else seemed aware of the sound, and was alarmed when it suddenly ceased. Had *I* heard it? No. Was I surprised by her tale? Not for one second. Over the years I have lost count of the number of times I have been asked those same questions on that very spot – the entrance to the sixteenth-century ruin, Mar's Wark. Spectral accounts of weeping bairns are, of course, common within the folk-record: at least three sites within the Old Town regularly boast similar reports. The dense verdant sprawl between two of these – Argyll's Ludging, on Castle Wynd, and the ruinous Cowane's House, in St Mary's Wynd – is a playground for local foxes whose baleful bleating might easily (and unsettlingly) be mistaken for that of an anguished tot. Mar's Wark, standing in the shadow of the Holy Rude Church, might well be similarly vexed by vulpine visitors – until recent renovations, the neighbouring cemetery was an equally overgrown boscage. Local tradition, however, provides a more sinister possibility.

The fragmented façade of the Wark – 'wark', incidentally, signifies a particularly impressive piece of building work, though John W. Small, in *The Ludgings of the Earl of Mar*, notes that this particular property was known locally as Mar's Ludging prior to brief seventeenth-century service as a workhouse – looms over Broad Street like some great shattered monument of former glory. Fittingly so. Its crumbling crenulations are all that remains of its founder's local legacy. The Erskines enjoyed a considerable status in the Scottish Court, serving as hereditary Keepers to Stirling Castle since the

Mar's Ludging, as seen from Broad Street. (David Kinnaird)

time of King David II. In 1542, the then keeper, John Erskine, personally escorted the six-year-old Mary, Queen of Scots to the safety of France during the destructive rampage of Henry VIII's 'Rough Wooing', loyally earning his title as 1st Earl of Mar in 1562, and the guardianship of the queen's heir, Prince James, the following year. Mary's forced abdication in 1567 increased his influence, and in 1571 he was appointed regent – the third to bear that burden during the boy's infancy. The first, Mary's half-brother James, 1st Earl of Moray, was assassinated in 1570. The second, Matthew Stewart, 4th Earl of Lennox, the prince's paternal grandfather, was accidentally shot (by his own men) during a pro-Marian raid on Stirling a year later. We'll get to the fourth shortly.

Mar's Wark, then, was not merely the townhouse of a provincial potentate, but a palace. Its wide façade, once three storeys high, has a central gateway flanked by octagonal towers adorned with the coats of arms of Mar and his countess. Courtiers, mermaids, gargoyles, mythological monsters and even – presumptuously adorning the upper gateway – the Royal Arms of Scotland, vie for attention amid the decorative pageant of its walls. There are curious quotes – biblical and poetic – and others more obscure in origin. A headless weatherworn figure on the north wall nearby the bound and surpliced image known as 'Jeannie Dark' (disputably 'Joan of Arc'), holds a book with an intriguingly cryptic inscription (now illegible) graven upon its open pages – 'TRA TOVR TYM / REVELL IT OVR CRYM' – 'Traitor Time revealed our crime'. It's an inscription the true meaning of which escapes even the scholarly Mr Small. Oddly, though, none have thought to directly link these words with one of the most curious and persistent legends associated with the site – a prophesy that Mar, his Wark and his heirs were cursed before the first foundations were laid, and which might hint as to the identity of the phantom tot.

The tale goes something like this. Queen Mary had been delivered of a child – James, a pale and sickly bairn – and Erskine was high in her favour, as one who had done her kindness in her youth. He was a familiar face, a friendly face, too – and the Catholic queen saw far too few of those. He was made guardian to the prince, but still he dreamed he might be something more. The opportunity to indulge his ambitions came when a wild-eyed servant roused him from his rest one night, warning that Mary's heir had not the strength to see the dawn. His thoughts, then, were all of duty – not duty to the queen, or to the realm he swore to serve, but to his own great name. Could not another babe be found to fill poor James' crib? One born from good, proud Erskine stock, perhaps? The other, the royal brat, might be hidden away within the foundations of his fine new mansion, which was then in the early stages of construction. A crime? No. Surely it was an act of kindness, for that act would spare the Scots the strife a war of succession would surely bring. That his own bloodline might be well advanced was but an added bonus. And so the deed was done.

When Mary fell, driven from her throne by her own folly and imprisoned by her English cousin Elizabeth I for conspiracy to end her life and sieze her throne, Mar promised her that the prince's charge would fall to him and him alone, and he would be true to that oath if to no other. In time he took the regent's reigns, and so could guide the king's young hand and shape him to his will. But, on the very day that he was set to take that office, he was confronted at the Alloa Tower by a stranger, a ragged man wrapped in what might once have been the vestments of a friar. This scarecrow had a message, a prophesy:

'TRA TOVR TYM REVELL IT OVR CRYM' – but what crime? Regicide? Infanticide? (David Kinnaird)

The entrance to Mar's Wark, and the graveyard beyond.
A ghostly baby's cries are regularly reported here.
(David Kinnaird)

The changeling – actress Nicole Lahbib, as Countess
Mar, tells her tale to a GhostWalk Audience in 1994.
(David Kinnaird)

Proud Chief of Mar, thou shalt be raised still higher, until thou sittest in the place of the King. Thou shalt rule and destroy, and thy work shall be after thy name, but thy work shall be the emblem of thy house, and shall teach mankind that he who cruelly and haughtily raiseth himself upon the ruins of the Holy cannot prosper. Thy work shall be cursed and shall never be finished. But thou shalt have riches and greatness, and shall be true to thy sovereign, and shall raise his banner in the field of blood. Then, when thou seemest to be highest, when thy power is mightiest, then shall come thy fall; low shall be thy head amongst the noblest of the people. Deep shall be thy moans among the children of dool [sorrow]. Thy lands shall be given unto the stranger, and thy titles shall lie among the dead … Thou, proud head and daggered hand, must dree thy weird, until horses be stabled in thy hall, and a weaver shall throw his shuttle in thy chamber of state …

Erskine sneered, and cast the ragged rascal from his door. He had no time for Papist threats. Was not England's queen a maid? With no heir of her own she'd surely seek a Union of the Crowns. His changeling might take the throne of England, too. But for all his boastful pride, for all his schemes, he would not see the glories that he craved. Mar sickened, his flesh worn out, they said, by selfless service to the Crown; his Wark, unfinished as he passed from this world; his heirs – his legal heirs – a rascal multitude. And James, his changeling, deprived of a mother's love, became his father's son – as proud and cruel as any Erskine lord.

Powerful stuff. The prophesy was astonishingly accurate, too, in its chronicling of Erskine misfortunes. Received wisdom has it that it was Cambuskenneth's abbot who uttered this 'Curse of Alloa Tower' – quoted here from T.F. Thiselton Dyer's delightfully odd *Strange Pages from Family Papers*, and oft-repeated (Drysdale, in *Old Faces, Old Places and Old Stories of Stirling*, is vehement in his conviction of its veracity). Erskine did 'rule and destroy', having, as Dyer puts it, 'commanded the destruction of Cambuskenneth Abbey, and took its stones to build himself a palace'. True. Might the motto above the rear entrance to the Wark – 'ESSPY SPEIK FVRTH AND SPAIR NOTHT / CONSIDDIR VEIL I CAIR NOTHT' ('If you speak forth and spare not / consider well I care not') – be a curt rebuke to his ecclesiastical critic? The Wark was never finished, serving as a makeshift barracks and stables in the seventeenth century, and was the Burgh workhouse by the middle of the eighteenth. But, as is so often the case, all is not quite what it seems.

The opening statement – 'thou shalt be raised still higher, until thou sittest in the place of the King' – might be taken to refer to Mar's elevation from guardian to regent, but could equally apply to the changeling myth that a Mar did literally sit in the place of the king. I've encountered many older residents of Castlehill who swear blind that the skeleton of a baby – 'wee King James himself' – was unearthed in the ruin if not within their own lifetimes, then within those of their own parents or grandparents. Could it be that the cryptic legend 'Traitor Time revealed our crime' was tacit acknowledgement that the dead prince's remains would ultimately be discovered as the building degraded, its woeful weeping (like Poe's 'Tell-Tale Heart') an insistent reminder of past infamy? If so, then it is curious that this epoch-altering discovery has so miraculously escaped reference even in the accounts of the parochial press.

But what of the 'curse' – accurate in so many other respects? The clue, I think – and it is far from subtle – lies in the comment that 'a weaver shall throw his shuttle in thy chamber of state'. Ah! A reference not to the *Regent* Mar, but to his dithering descendant, the Jacobite 6th Earl – known as 'Bobbing John' on account of his tendency to bob, like a weaver's shuttle, from faction to faction (Tory to Whig, Hanoverian to Jacobite). John's inconstancy cost him dearly at the Battle of Sheriffmuir, during the Rising of 1715: his confiscated lands were 'given unto the stranger', and his titles were revoked. Despite Dyer's claim of the curse's 'boast of great antiquity', I can find no reference to it prior to Bobbing John's disgrace at Sheriffmuir, and it was not transcribed until the Victorian era. No wonder it is so accurate – it is an exercise in political spin, written long after the events it described. For all his faults – as a shrewd and occasionally ruthless political operator, he had many – the 1st Earl was true to his promise to Queen Mary that he would never relinquish his protection of her heir without her consent, even following her imprisonment. He was still guardian to young King James when he died in 1572.

This, of course, is perplexing in itself. The Wark's oft-reported wailing babe may not be any *known* victim of regicide or infanticide, but – theories regarding wayward wildlife aside – its true identity remains an intriguing mystery.

Auld Staney Breeks

John Cowane's Hospital

A smug stone figure, the work of seventeenth-century master mason John Mill, peers from a plinth above the entrance to John Cowane's Hospital – a fine example of Scottish Renaissance architecture, its E-shaped plan dignified by an elegant four-storey central tower. He poses proudly, as though approving the white harled walls and rich strapwork decorations adorning the pediments above its high windows. As well he might. This is, after all, the enduring legacy of Stirling's greatest benefactor, and – according to legend – Cowane is the only one of its apparitions whose spectral manifestations can be included on Stirling's social calendar.

If the Tolbooth in Broad Street is the Old Town's heart, then the John Cowane has been periodically providing the Burgh with life-sustaining CPR for many years. It is perhaps curious, given that he was a councillor, a merchant, a banker, Dean of Guild (a civic office second only to that of Provost), and a Commissioner to the Scots Parliament, that we know so little about this gentleman – though the facts that are available paint a colourful picture. He came from a distinguished merchant family, funding a number of his more speculative business ventures through part-ownership of three privateers – the *Gift of God*, the *George of Queensferry* and the *Grace of Dysart* – which plundered foreign ships, and was a shrewd, savvy political player on the national

Cowane's Hospital – as seen from the Old Kirkyard. Building was interrupted by two 'visitations' of the plague. (David Kinnaird)

Dedication on the tower of Cowane's Hospital. (David Kinnaird)

and local stage. It is Cowane's exertions in other areas, however, which have assured his reputation. Like many figures famed for their public virtues, bold John is better known for his private passions – though, surprisingly, only one account of his many rumoured conquests survives in Stirling's records:

> 8 August 1611, Kirk Session Minutes. The quilk day compeirit Agnes Cowane, servand to Duncan Patersone and confessit fornication with John Cowane, Merchand, and that the first and last tyme was all ye monet imediatelie preceding the feast of Witsonday last. The brethrein continewis [furder] with her quile ye said Jonne be also tried.

The price of the famed fornicator's folly? £6 Scots, and an appointment to sit upon the Penance Stool in the Holy Rude Church upon the 'nixt sex sermon days', that the whole Burgh might see his shame and show him scorn. As John G. Harrison notes in his comprehensive Stirling Council study, 'The World of John Cowane', three sittings was the standard penalty, so at twice that tariff, this was probably not a 'first offence'.

In 1615, the boisterous burgess had another 'first and last tyme' encounter (outdoors this time) with one Christian McGibbon of Menteith. A daughter was delivered of this fleeting fancy, and penance made – but this was in another parish (Callendar) – and of little concern to John's neighbours. The Burgh's most notorious bachelor never married, and bequeathed the bulk of his huge fortune – 40,000 Merks (around £2,222 Sterling) – to endow an almshouse for the 'succour of 12 decayed Gildbrothers'. This was Cowane's Hospital, constructed between 1637 and 1649 (building being interrupted by two 'visitations' of the plague and one Civil War). Much of the stonework was fashioned from the ruins of the long-abandoned Cambuskenneth Abbey, leading local gossips to sneer that desecration was the cause of delays and the illness at the town. Pensioners were provided with 40 Scots Shillings, accommodation and heating, but strictly forbidden female company. Cowane, if nothing else, had a keen sense of irony. The hospital was used as barracks during Cromwell's occupation, and has served as the Burgh's Guildhall since 1724. The Cowane Trust, which continues to manage its benefactor's estate, is still based within the building.

Mill's statue holds court over the main entrance, and is host to Stirling's most enduring supernatural story. On the stroke of midnight each Hogmanay (New Year's Eve), Cowane's spirit is said to rise from its last resting place in the nearby churchyard and enter his still, stone effigy. This graven golem then jerks to life, leaping gaily from its plinth – dancing his wayward way through the streets, no doubt in search of the same fair female flesh that Cowane was so partial to in life. Though Cowane's is, as I say, the best known 'haunting' in Stirling, I have yet to encounter any sober citizen of the Castle Crag who has encountered his 'party spirit'. Having experience of Stirling during the holiday season, I fear it is the priapic phantom himself who should beware: the bonnie lassies of the modern Burgh are more than a match for him. The statue and spirit are both known locally as 'Auld Staney Breeks' (Old Stone – or dirty – Trousers), supposedly on account of the mottled weather-worn paintwork upon the effigy's apparel. Given that his amorous reputation has endured as long as his beneficence, it may also be a warning to other like-minded statesmen that if they are not careful how they conduct themselves in this world, they may still be washing their dirty laundry in the next.

A Hanged Man?

Cowane's House, St Mary's Wynd

While the seasonal spectre of Cowane is almost certainly little more than an amusing invention, he has a connection – albeit tangential – to another anomalous experience within the town with which I was personally involved. As mentioned in Chapter One, I accompanied a group of Edinburgh psychics around the sights of Stirling one drear, dark night in November 2007. For the most part, our magical history tour led us to locations with time-honoured supernatural traditions. One had no such legacy. My inner-sceptic was eager, I suppose, to see just how suggestible these so-called sensitives

'Auld Staney Breeks' – Stirling's very own party spirit, whose wraith inhabits this cold clay every Hogmanay (31 December). (David Kinnaird)

John Cowane's grave, restored in the nineteenth century. (David Kinnaird)

might be, by introducing a 'control' site with no apparent history of being haunted – but with every appearance of seeming so. A foul night, it was with much relief that the group noticed two warm and welcoming historic taverns – Whistlebinkies (occupying the former King's Stables) and the Settle Inn – within sight of our final stop, John Cowane's House, in St Mary's Wynd.

Known to older locals as 'Queen Mary's Palace', the building has absolutely no connection with the infamous and unfortunate Queen of Scots, though the Revd Dr Charles Rogers – the Victorian nationalist and antiquary who worked so diligently to secure support for the erection of the National Wallace Monument – believed the property to have been the residence of James Douglas, 4th Earl of Morton, fourth (and final) regent to Mary's heir, James VI. Unlikely: a writ relating to a neighbouring property a decade earlier declares the site as 'the land of the deceased John Cowane', grandsire to Stirling's benefactor. The intertwined initials, IC:AC, adorning a courtyard dormer, commemorate a 1633 expansion of the property by John and his sister, Agnes. J.S. Fleming, in *Old Nooks of Stirling*, concedes that there is no doubt 'something in the suggestion of its remains showing an ancient magnificence attributable to the occupancy of a person of greater rank than a mere merchant burgess'.

'Queen Mary's Palace' – Cowane's House, as seen from the dismal huddle of St Mary's Wynd in 1870. (Picture reproduced by kind permission of the Smith Art Gallery & Museum)

It is easy to underestimate just how impressive and imposing this ramshackle ruin must once have been – three storeys high, extending 100ft from the Mediaeval Vennel of le Virgin Marie, and boasting gables 5ft thick. It once incorporated a banqueting hall and a chapel (to St Mary's Well, which gave the street its name). Some sense of its scale is revealed through reference to The Hearth Tax, levied in 1691 on all fireplaces. A weaver's home had one; a merchant's two or three; Cowane's House – then the property of the Schorts, merchant heirs to Agnes, her brother having died without (legitimate) progeny – had twelve. By the middle of the following century, Stirling was in decline, and the former mansion was a workshop – sold by the creditors of Messrs Scott and Gilfillan's Carpet House Co. to Patrick Connall, whose heirs leased it to the town in 1776, 'for behoof of the community of the said Burgh and for the purposes of schools and accommodating the masters thereof.' Derelict by 1870, it was unroofed by the Town Council, and despite Fleming's gloomy 1898 prediction that 'in a very few years time very little of its walls will survive to indicate their original character,' it *has* endured – another towering spectre bemoaning a Burgh bereft of former glories.

Rarely subject to the public gaze, it looks every inch the forbidding 'haunted house' – the sort of desolate, rough-hewn place where even the most sceptical of souls might imagine dangers lurking in every weathered nook and cranny. This is why it has long been a dramatic port-of-call on the Stirling GhostWalk, and why, that damp and dismal November eve, I unlocked its rusted metal gate and bid my psychic companions enter.

Most did not wish to linger long – though, truth be told, that probably owed more to the cruel Caledonian climate (and the proximity of a tasty pint) than to any sense of psychic pressure. The site's only supernatural associations, as far as I was aware, were vague (and increasingly rare) reports of a crying baby heard near the courtyard – and spread, no doubt, by parents eager to dissuade their reckless progeny from using 'The Palace' as a playground. These, according to local lore, were the wails of one of Auld Staney Breeks' bastard bairns, hastily drowned in the kitchen well. Not very likely: the beneficent burgess was far too brazen to resort to such a risky stratagem. His known 'legal heirs' – note the term 'legal' rather than 'legitimate' – survived to adulthood. The responses of one gentleman in our party – the same whose Condemned Cell comments had intrigued me in the Tolbooth – were interesting. Standing in the gardens behind the courtyard he became suddenly nauseous, his head reeling, his breath laboured – and, as we helped him out into the reassuring street-lighting of St Mary's Wynd, I thought to dismiss him as nothing more than another victim of that peculiarly selective claustrophobia so often experienced by imaginative night-visitors to old buildings.

Of course, were Dr Rogers' theories regarding residence (if not ownership) by the regent Morton in the 1570s valid, then there *might* be what Fleming terms a 'tragic interest' to this tale; it would have been in the banqueting hall which once stood in those same overgrown gardens that John Stewart, Lord Chancellor of Scotland – who had incautiously accused his spiteful host of complicity in the murder of his royal charge's father, Lord Darnley – was poisoned in April 1579.

Reference to more recent records reminded me of another incident which might reflect some light on the psychic's experience. It told of a poor, sad soul, a local prison officer (whose details I will not include here, in consideration of the sensitivities of relatives still resident within the town) driven to distraction by the 'black dog' of depression, who had clambered into the long-abandoned rear of the property, intent upon taking his own life in that forgotten place. Despairingly, he tied a cord to a high branch within that lonely arbour, coiled the other end about his throat, and jumped. Hanging is a notoriously treacherous mechanism of self-destruction, even when professionally executed – as the tale of the aged Alan Mair illustrates – and it seems that this fellow's hopes for a hasty end were in vain. The drop was insufficient for his neck to snap, and he was left to slowly strangle. A horrific end – his head reeling, unable to draw breath, consumed by despair – just as the gentleman from Edinburgh had described. Thankfully his is not an experience shared by other visitors to the 'Palace'.

A few stern words from J.S. Fleming:

> Whoever is to blame, the neglected condition of this ancient mansion certainly reflects on the gentlemen who have represented, and those who presently represent, the institution John Cowane founded, and on the town's people who so largely benefitted for many years by his handsome provision for them; while it is little less than a scandal on the town itself.

As true today as it was in 1898.

The interior of Cowane's House, and the gardens in which suicide and possibly murder occurred. (David Kinnaird)

Unfortunate Argyll

Argyll's Ludging, Mar Place

Argyll's Ludging, the most complete extant example of a seventeenth-century Scottish townhouse, has long been one of the castle's most stately satellites. A tower house stood on this site from at least the middle of the sixteenth century, lavishly converted and expanded in the 1630s by Sir William Alexander of Menstrie, Master of Requests and Keeper of the Signet to King James VI (I). James's courtly 'Philosophical Poet' was instrumental in establishing the colony of New Scotland (Nova Scotia), for which he earned the title Viscount Canada. His coat of arms, complete with mermaid and winged Mercury, still exotically adorns the main entrance. Further expansion – the creation of a spectacular rectangular courtyard, and the addition of conical French corner turrets and interior wall decorations – occurred during the short residence of Archibald Campbell, 9th Earl of Argyll, from the early 1670s. The Leigh Hall, state rooms and kitchens have been lavishly restored to the grandeur they enjoyed during the occupancy of that troubled Chieftain of the Clan Campbell. The building served as an army hospital and as overspill barracks for the Argyll and Sutherland Highlanders, stationed at Stirling Castle, from the nineteenth century, and as the town's SYHA Youth Hostel prior to the restoration of the Erskine Marykirk in the latter years of the twentieth. Maintained by Historic Scotland, access is by guided tour only (contact Stirling Castle for details – www.stirlingcastle.gov.uk).

The site was visited by Brian Allan and a team from Strange Phenomena Investigations, on 19 September 1999. Here they were accompanied by a seasoned and knowledgeable Historic Scotland guide, Gary D'Arcy. D'Arcy was careful not to provide these unfamiliar visitors with comments or information which might influence their findings – I have focussed here on those impressions which may have relevance to characters and incidents from the site's known historical record.

In the Old Kitchen, medium Anne-Marie Sneddon had a sense of sickness and nausea. There had, she was sure, been a great many deaths in the building over a long period. This was a feeling shared by her psychic colleagues, both here and in the courtyard. Jim Lochhead complained of toothache – a sympathetic suggestion, he felt, that the building had been used as a hospital of some kind. It had indeed. It served as medical quarters for more than a century, tending injured Argylls through the trauma and tribulations of many conflicts. Sneddon's vision of a chain-mailed and armoured martial figure standing guard by the grand fireplace in the New Kitchens is more difficult to tie to the known history of the house, as neither mail nor plate armour was particularly commonplace by the time of Alexander or Argyll. That this grim figure might be in some way associated with an earlier incident from the site's history cannot, of course, be dismissed. Nor can Anne-Marie's belief that a devastating fire may have required the restoration of a structure here in the past – much of Stirling was razed during the Douglas raids of the 1450s, after all (*see* Chapter 4).

Still in the New Kitchen, Jim became aware of the presence of a distraught and distracted male energy, consumed by 'madness' while involved with some clandestine scheme.

The entrance to Argyll's Ludging looms over Castle Wynd in the eighteenth century. (Picture reproduced by kind permission of the Smith Art Gallery & Museum)

The spirit was possessed by an overpowering sense of guilt: he had escaped danger, but his plotting had not gone according to plan, and others had paid the price for his actions. Collusion and conspiracy would certainly have been no strangers to the Ludging – though not necessarily to its kitchens. Archibald had inherited the earldom in 1663, two years after his father had been executed as a traitor by Charles II. Though he shared little of his goodsire's Covenanting political passion, the 9th Earl was never to escape the consequences of his father's crime – his life was constantly confounded by conflicts with the Macleans, the ambitious Earl of Middleton and by the personal quandary posed by the Test Bill of 1681, which imposed an obligation on the nobles who took it to conform to any religion the king pleased. This requirement – with Charles's Catholic brother, James, his most likely successor – troubled the Presbyterian Argyll.

He grudgingly accepted the oath – describing it as 'consistent with itself' – largely to quell gossip that he was a traitor like his father, but his hesitancy led to accusations and imprisonment for treason. A daring escape followed, and a catastrophic course of events was set in motion, leading to Argyll spearheading an abortive Highland rebellion against the newly-crowned James VII (II), in 1685. While it is true that Archibald was overtaken by the 'madness' of events, which fashioned him as a reluctant radical martyr, he did not escape. He was beheaded in Edinburgh's infamous 'Maiden' on Monday, 30 June 1685.

An escape of sorts is hinted at in a curious incident recently reported in the Ludging. Guide Sandy Easson recounts the tale of staff opening up the visitor attraction one morning and discovering the doors to the kitchens standing wide – the heavy iron lock having been removed. It was soon found, on the far side of the room, and a locksmith was called to repair the damage. He expressed no little consternation at what he found. These were curious vandals indeed, he said, who would dismantle a heavy lock, remove it from its mount, and then carefully reassemble it before unceremoniously dumping it in a corner. Prankster or poltergeist? You decide.

Having stayed many times at the Ludging as a teenager, when it served as a youth hostel, and performed here regularly prior to Historic Scotland's renovations, I was

The entrance to the Ludging, displaying the arms of William Alexander, Earl of Stirling. (Illustration by W. Lovett c. 1950)

*Castle Wynd – the façade of Argyll's Ludging.
(David Kinnaird)*

*What scared a young serviceman here in the
1950s? (Patricia Brannigan)*

surprised to find that others had been deliriously discommoded by this charming building. J. Docherty, a private in the Argylls who, quartered here between December 1955 and January 1957, had a most alarming tale to tell. A member of a regiment famed for its fury on the battlefield, and a self-styled 'Glasgow hard-man, afraid of nobody', Docherty was distraught by the fear which frequent phantasmal appearances in the room he shared with another soldier, Private Bothwell, prompted in him. The figure of an anxious wraith had become a regular visitor, and he was so alarmed by events that he jumped onto his motorbike and sped off to his native city (and into the arms of his teenage fiancée) at every opportunity, rising early to speed back to Stirling in time for roll-call. 'I think I was more afraid of my RSM, Skinner, than I was of the ghost,' he wrote in 1999. 'That's all that stopped me running away.' His quarters, described as 'very large for two privates in the days when soldiers slept in the castle in double bunk-beds', were located on the first floor, toward the rear of the north wing of the Ludging, where it intersects with the main building. The ghost would appear by the rear wall – 'not through the wall, but appearing inside my room' – and what little sleep the privates enjoyed was the result of the 'exhaustion of fear' at encountering this shadowy figure, who appeared to be in considerable distress. Looking back over the decades, the old soldier was convinced that his frightful visitor was connected in some way with the room behind the wall from which it emerged, then locked tight and unused. The identity of the alleged phantom is impossible to guess at – Docherty's description is vague – but reference to the Ordnance Survey map of 1858 reveals disconcerting data. The chamber in question appears at that time to have been the 'Dead House' – the hospital mortuary. Was the spirit who intruded upon the private's privacy 'unfortunate Argyll' – as he is said to have described himself on the way to execution – or some long-forgotten soldier? Who can say.

No such reports were made during the building's time as a hostel – the most frequently cited 'ghostly' disturbance during that era being the sound of a crying baby. Anne-Marie Sneddon made just such a report during the SPI visit to the property, though, as aforementioned, I believe the origins of these sounds are more likely to lie in the dense grasslands behind the Ludging than in any unquiet grave. These days, strange sensations and experiences in the busy visitor attraction are rare, though Archibald Campbell's glum ghost is still occasionally blamed for minor mishaps within his former home, such as 2009's failure of the Ludging's Christmas tree lights: guides joke that the irksome earl would be unlikely to approve of such festive frivolity.

three

The Graveyards and Gowan Hill

'No one in Scotland can escape from the past. It is everywhere, haunting like a ghost.'
Geddes MacGregor

'We must always await Life's Last Day', declares the Latin legend graven on the grand monument to Provost John McCulloch, who died in the Burgh in 1689, 'and no-one should be called Happy until he is Dead and Buried'. Fair enough. Death was, as Burns so sagely put it, 'the poor man's dearest friend, The kindest and the best … a blest relief for those / That weary-laden mourn!' ('Man Was Made To Mourn', 1784.) Those seeking eternal rest in the environs of Stirling's Holy Rude churchyard may have been better advised to look for other accommodations. Peace, here, was in seriously short supply.

The area surrounding the church has almost certainly been used for burials since at least the twelfth century, when a chapel was built by monks from Dunfermline Abbey. This original wooden structure was damaged by fire in 1406, then again in 1452 and 1455 – as part of the Clan Douglas's fiery revenge against James II for his betrayal and bloody murder of the Earl of Douglas. Supporters of the imprisoned Mary, Queen of Scots battled here with royal troops on 3 September 1571. Cromwell's forces did likewise during their assault in August 1650. The tower of the Kirk still shows the pockmarks of musket-shot and cannon-fire, as do many of the monuments: the Mort Clothed cadaver decorating the base of the 1636 stone, erected for his parents by local merchant John Service, almost seems to be cowering from the fearsome enfilade of General Monk's siege guns. Further blood and thunder ensued in 1746 when Charles Edward Stuart strove to reclaim the ancient seat of his forefathers. He failed – and the current ruination of Mar's Work, which sits in the shadow

The Service Stone – pockmarked by the musket-shot and cannon fire which has often disturbed the 'eternal rest' of Stirling's dead. (Patricia Brannigan)

of the Kirk, is as much the result of Bonnie Charlie's folly in placing his siege guns on the low ground surrounding Erskine's mansion, as it is of age, entropy or ancient ecclesiastical curses.

James Ronald, in *Landmarks of Old Stirling*, argues that executions were a 'permanent institution' here throughout the seventeenth century (one certainly occurred on a specially erected 'Gallous', in 1652, but the 'Gallous Mailing' beyond the 'Barras Yett', or Burgh Gate – now home to the Victorian Black Boy Fountain, in Park Lane – is a more likely location during this era). It is often said that as many here died above ground than were ever buried beneath: a jest that is probably not too far from the truth. Modern visitors (and residents) are, thankfully, able to enjoy a little more peace and quiet in this pretty parkland – renovated by Stirling Council in 2008-9, at a cost of £1.7 million. This comparative calm in recent years may, of course, explain the sharp decline of spirit sightings in the Holy Rude, Valley and Ballengeich kirkyards. Unsurprisingly, the turbulent histories of these burial grounds have played their part in shaping the supernatural tales associated with them.

The Black Lady

A local woman – now in middle age, and a volunteer at Stirling's Smith Art Gallery & Museum – had a curious and unnerving experience as she pushed her pram along the rough pathway of the Back Walk one autumn afternoon in the early 1970s. Then a young mother, she could hear only the gleeful gurgling of the tot as she trundled through the twilight over the cascade of brittle, brown leaves covering the path – which circles the cemetery and Castle Rock, and marks the line of the Burgh defences fortified by Mary de Guise in the 1540s. As she reached the steep incline from Cowane's Hospital to the Ladies' Hill she paused to catch her breath, and was startled to feel something 'like a finger pressing up and down the length of my back'. She turned, and was alarmed to find herself alone upon the shadowy path. She lost no time in hurrying home.

Such encounters here were once common-place, it seems, and attributed to visitations of the Black Lady, a ghostly nun, supposedly seeking furtive union with her secret priestly lover in some secluded nook of the Castle Rock. Given the infuriatingly anonymous nature of many of Stirling's phantoms, it would

The Back Walk – line of the Burgh's defences, and a favourite haunt of the Black Lady. (David Kinnaird)

only be fair to note that the bad habits attributed to her probably owe a great deal more to the violently anti-Catholic sentiments once so rife within the town, than they do to any actual fleshly transgressions.

The Protestant Church of the Holy Rude, and Ebenezer Erskine's austere presbytery, the Erskine Marykirk – now the local SYHA hostel – loom over the line of the Walk, and many of the 'guid Kirk-men' of the town would seize any opportunity to scorn the sinful ways of Stirling's Papist past. The Royal Commission on the Ancient and Historical Monuments of Scotland does note that James II founded a Greyfriars (Franciscan) Convent in Stirling in 1449, on the site occupied in 1856 by the Victorian High School (a hotel since 1991). Greyfriars was destroyed during the religious and civic strife of the 1550s. Its lands – including a slaughterhouse – also extended along the line of the Back Walk, as far as the Old Town Jail. So, while the particulars of the Black Lady's tale resist detailed scrutiny, encountering a surpliced figure on this leafy lane would not have been an unlikely prospect. James Ronald notes, in *Landmarks of Old Stirling*, that the nuns of North Berwick nearly came to blows with the Dunfermline Dominicans who established the original Holy Rude and Chapel Royal in Stirling in 1220, over tithes due from the parishes of Airthrey and Cornton, so perhaps the Black Lady's haste is for arbitration, not amour.

A stubbornly silent and uncommunicative spirit – none of Stirling's female phantoms have a great deal to say for themselves – her purpose is as obscure as her origin and destination, though she is generally thought by older locals to be a herald of ill omen, creating a sense of dread appropriate to the shadowy, overgrown causeway she frequents. Sightings are rare since the path was paved and electric light added, though uncanny encounters on the outskirts of the churchyard still occur. On the afternoon of 30 November (St Andrew's Day) 2002, Rab Allan, Master of Works for the Cowane Trust, had one such unsettling experience. At the foot of the stone steps leading to the summit

Ebenezer Erskine's tomb – Erskine's church overlooks the Back Walk where the Black Lady is said to appear. (David Kinnaird)

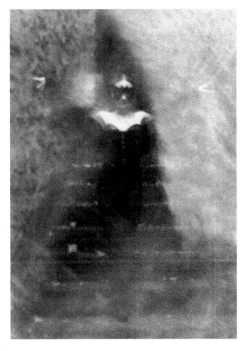

The Black Lady – the Stirling Ghost Walk's Patricia Brannigan – prowls, 2002. (Promotional image by David Kinnaird)

of the Ladies' Hill, where a rough path leads down to the Back Walk, he spied a figure in what appeared to be a capacious grey coat with a high collar or hood, hurrying up the path from the Valley. A local, who has lived and worked around the cemetery all his life, and who has no truck with 'silly superstitions', he was about to call a cheery welcome – sure that the grey man was me, garbed in the great grey postal-cloak which forms part of my Staffman's livery – though he did think it odd that a Ghost Walk should be in progress so early in the day. What happened next silenced him before he could utter a word, as the figure 'just vanished into the stone at the top of the path. Not behind. Not beside. Straight through. Into the stone.' (I, incidentally, have a saintly alibi for the time of this odd encounter: I was playing Santa Claus in a local shopping centre all day.) Could this have been the Black Lady's immortal *inamorta* – a Franciscan Greyfriar in his distinctive vestments – hurrying to meet her under some secluded bower?

The Pink Lady

The castle's Green Lady (*see* Chapter 4) is said to be a frequent visitor to the Holy Rude's churchyards. Interviewed for the *Sightings* television show in 1992, a number of local residents recounted youthful encounters with that celebrated spectre.

'She wasn't actually on the ground,' said Marion Fairley, 'she was kind of floating, but she had her face away from me. But it definitely was a woman.' Dennis Roberts' experience was more dramatic:

> What we saw just at the corner of the graveyard, up at the foot of the castle wall, was a Green Lady. A lady dressed in green … Seven or eight of us ran up to see what was going on. Covering twenty-five yards, there was nobody in either direction.

Rab Roberts' vision of 'a shadow. No face … just a dark shadow in the corner' might, of course, apply equally to the Black Lady as the Green – and there does appear to be considerable confusion sometimes in distinguishing the Burgh's female spirits. 'It makes you cold,' said Mr Roberts, 'but I know what I saw.' Knowing what – or who – you saw in supernatural Stirling isn't always easy.

Consider the Pink Lady, the only one of the Old Town's many reported revenants to warrant a mention in Antony D. Hippisley Coxe's *Haunted Britain*: 'a young girl dressed in pink silk and surrounded by a pink light' who 'walks between the castle and the church, near Lady's Rock, once the point of vantage where womenfolk watched their men jousting.' Martin Coventry, in *Haunted Castles & Houses of Scotland*, mentions her as having been identified (though how I can't imagine) as Mary, Queen of Scots – like the castle's more famous Green Lady – or the servant who reputedly saved her from her burning bower, or a lovelorn local maiden who lost her beau to Longshanks' siege of 1304 (though, as Geoff Holder notes in *The Guide to Mysterious Stirlingshire*, this is 'a date too early for pink silk'). The stern rocky promontory of the Ladies' Rock – or Ladies' Hill – does indeed overlook the orderly Valley Cemetery, fashioned in 1857 from the area known as the 'Tournament Ground', where jousting, duelling and other courtly blood-sports were reputed to have once been played out at a safe distance from the delicate damsels seated on the hill. It was also used, with less pomp but rather more purpose, when the Burgh Council declared that the weekly horse market be 'keipit an halden in the Valey an in na uther place of this town', in 1646. A pink 'aura' is often said to indicate a spiritual predisposition to romance or desire, and the Pink Lady's appearances, according to tradition, were often presaged by an appropriately feminine scent of blossom and a lingering sense of longing. It is worth remembering, though, that the colour had no particular gender-specific associations prior to the end of the eighteenth century, so the shrouded pink figure may not be a 'lady' at all.

The connection with the ill-starred Queen of Scots – whose spectre seems to be a far more active *habitué* of her nation's historic sites in spectral form than she ever was in life – is curious. Though oft-repeated in print, it is almost entirely absent from local anecdotal lore. During early performances of the Stirling GhostWalk, I was warned by one stern old lady living in St Mary's Wynd that my fellow performers and I 'shouldna' fash the Quine' if we came upon her – that we shouldn't upset the young woman – who, in *her* understanding, was a mournful mother who had lost her child to illness and was searching for the bairn's long-forgotten resting place. This would, of course, explain her restlessness and the feeling of great sadness that her visitations are said to cause. Others confidently identified her with an occupant of the grave beneath one of the most striking stones in the Old Kirkyard.

The tomb in question grandly marks the lair belonging to tradesman James Livingston, brother-in-law to its most infamous occupant – Mary Witherspoon (*née* Stevenson), the fifty-five-year-old widow of stonemason James Witherspoon, who died of dropsy (edema) on 16 November 1822.

The Pink Lady – actress Janet Lascalles assumes the mantle of Mistress Witherspoon in the 1997 Stirling GhostWalk. (Promotional image by David Kinnaird and Alan Murray)

From Burgh records, Witherspoon's life and experience seem no more or less dramatic than those of most middle-aged matrons of her class and era, yet many visitors to the howff are quickly drawn to her grave – particularly those who claim some mediumistic ability. That the monument should so readily catch the eye is no surprise; it certainly is dramatic. Its central image – most likely salvaged from a much older monument – shows a grimly shrouded Death wielding a sexton's spade and staff, pressing a flailing female figure back into the earth. The message is clear enough. Resistance is futile: 'all flesh is grass' to the Grim Reaper.

On the frosty morning of 22 November 1822, a grim discovery was made amid the cluttered stony sprawl of the kirkyard: a sight sure to strike terror into any faithful heart. The earth around the Livingstone lair, where Mistress Witherspoon had been planted only three days past, was sunken and scattered – the pit a gaping maw. It seemed certain that the horror that had for so long plagued the churchyards of our capital had come, at last, to Stirling: 'Resurrection Men', raising the newly-dead so that they might be sliced, diced and studied by the anatomists of the universities. That the dissections performed by these learned gentlemen – who might pay as much as £12 for an interesting specimen – were intended to better the lot of all mankind was small comfort. The faithful of the town soon scrambled in the dirt to satisfy themselves that the resting places of their own dear-departed had not been similarly defiled. How could a body

A female figure struggles against Death on the grave of Mary Witherspoon. (Patricia Brannigan)

Stirling GhostWalk actress Patricia Brannigan as the unfortunate Mary Witherspoon, thought by some to be the Pink Lady. (Photograph by Patricia Brannigan)

subjected to such butchery rise anew at the Last Trump's call? For God-fearing folk, the grave-robbers' greatest crime was not theft – but their depriving the dead of the Great Resurrection promised in scripture.

When it was discovered that the ghoul responsible for the crime was James McNab – the very gravedigger who had buried the widow, and whose presence in the kirkyard, day or night, spade in hand, none would ever have thought to question – their distress was doubled. Cornered, he cockily confessed his crime. With Daniel Mitchell, a schoolmaster, he had sought to steal the corpse for sale to local medical student, John Forrest. Forrest had fled to the continent as soon as the crime was discovered, and the villains were ordered into the foul cells beneath the court to await redrafting of the indictment against them. Instead, much to their surprise – and *relief*, as they would almost certainly hang – they were released, in error. They had cheated death, but their surly smugness as they sauntered through the streets was to be short-lived. In fury at the incompetence of the courts, the townsfolk elected upon a more visceral and immediate exercise of justice. Within the hour an outraged mob – armed with stones, sticks and cudgels – stormed McNab's lodgings behind the old Corn Exchange Inn (now the modern extension to the Municipal Buildings). Others raided Mitchell's rooms, forcing him to flee across the rooftops. Soon the pair were cowering in the cells once more, as angry citizens advanced on the Tolbooth. The castle garrison were called upon to aid the town's only policeman in the prisoners' defence. One nervous squaddie – rather the worse for drink – discharged his weapon at the crazed crowd converging on Jail Wynd. As another was struck down, a full-scale riot ensued – the townsfolk's sticks and stones set against the bayonets and rifle-butts of the troops as they battled up and down St John Street. Miraculously, no fatalities occurred.

The fate of the pair is uncertain. Their names do not appear in records of executions – surprising, as theirs was certainly a capital crime. The instigator of their wrongdoing, John Forrest, was eventually elevated to the post of Inspector-General of Hospitals, his career clearly untainted by past criminal associations.

Being men of good family and noble intent, surgeons were rarely brought-to-book for their complicity in (and encouragement of) this ghoulish trade, and often benefited from it – as hanged felons routinely found their flesh given over to doctors for dissection and study. The gallows was, indeed, one of the few legal sources of surgical specimens prior to the Anatomy Act of 1832. This was the fate of Ulsterman William Burke who, with his partner (and ultimate betrayer) William Hare, has become synonymous with the crime of grave-robbing – despite *never* having disinterred a single corpse.

Burke and Hare were murderers; serial-killers preying upon Edinburgh's weak and destitute. Burke's common-law wife, Helen M'Dougal, was of Stirling stock, and may indeed have been resident in the town at the time of the Burgh's own body-snatching outrage. Whatever their fate, Mitchell and McNab were spared Helen's husband's inglorious end: hanged at the capital's Grassmarket on 28 January 1829, then dissected at the Edinburgh Medical College. Portions of his flesh were sold off at public auction to patrons eager to have a macabre memento of the famously foul fellow. One small portion – reverently framed and labelled – is currently in the care of the Smith Art Gallery & Museum.

A patch of Edinburgh body-snatcher William Burke's skin. (Picture reproduced by kind permission of the Smith Art Gallery & Museum)

Its donor, Dr Alex Paterson of Bridge of Allan, writing in 1890, recounted an unnerving experience relating to another choice morsel of the murderer's hide:

> When I was attending the University of Edinburgh a fellow student got a piece of Burke's skin, and covered his fishing book with it. One day he was fishing on a loch from a boat in the North when a violent storm of wind and rain arose which lasted for some time. The book, which was lying on one of the seats of the boat, was suddenly swept away by a great gust of wind, and the storm thereafter immediately ceased. The boatman, a Highlander, said he was very glad the Devil had taken the book away, and saved them from being drowned.

Dr Paterson is also the likely donor of a peculiar fur-trimmed hat which, according to one grim local tradition, either belonged to Burke or was fashioned (in part) from his scalp. This is not as outlandish a prospect as it might initially appear. The doctor notes: 'The bodies of the guillotined in Paris were skinned and the skins tanned, and chiefly used for making leather breeches and straps for the soldiers. Female skins, being thinner, were principally used for making gloves.' Could the cap have adorned a morbidly inclined fashionista? Possibly – though the reddish brown fur seems more likely to indicate that the skin (like the tale) is rabbit.

Burke's widow returned to Stirling, albeit briefly, after the unpleasantness in Edinburgh, and took up with a spinner named Campbell, with whom she travelled to Perth's Deanstone Cotton Mill to seek employment. After only three days there her past caught up with her. A Glasgow broadside, dated 25 April 1829, tells that she was …

Above: *According to one local legend, the fur trim on this cap was fashioned from the scalp of William Burke. (Picture reproduced by kind permission of the Smith Art Gallery & Museum)*

Right: *One of the Holy Rude's many decorative Victorian monuments. (David Kinnaird)*

… attacked by a great number of Individuals, most of them Females, who attacked her furiously, siezed her by the hair of the head and strangled her, one of the women dispatched her by putting her foot on her breast, and crushed her severely.

The passions prompted by Mary Witherspoon's post-mortem fate were no less fevered. Her heir, a simple-minded lad known locally as Daft Jamie, was so distraught by the events following his mother's disinterment that he took his own life (or died of a broken heart – depending on accounts), and the grave-robbing had a lasting effect on the Burgh: armed guards continued to patrol the churchyard by night for many months, and a watchtower was erected nearby John Cowane's Hospital to aid their vigil. Perhaps, her eternal rest having been so soon – and so brutally – disturbed, or distraught by the violence, venom and injustice that the event provoked, the spirit of the stonemason's wife is unable to find rest. Perhaps this spirit – rarely reported these days – was in some way a manifestation of this civil strife.

'The Millhall Ghost'

A similarly strife-related spectre is mentioned by Alfred G. Reilly, a frequent contributor to the *Stirling Observer, Stirling Journal, Stirling Sentinel* and a host of other local and national journals for more than sixty years. In his 1948 series 'A Newspaperman Looks Back: Stories of 25 Years', published in the *Stirling Sentinel*, Alf reported the curious experiences of quarrymen and miners from the nearby Millhall pits in 1926. A strange figure in white had been observed regularly on the roads coming to and from the pit, often in the hours between 9 p.m. and midnight. The thought that this might simply have been a drover from one of the many local farms, his distinctive white coverall flapping as he sought to retrieve some stubbornly independent-minded sheep, was considered, but quickly dismissed.

These were hard men. Superstitious, perhaps – as many whose occupations are so famously perilous often are – but unlikely to be frequently deceived by so commonplace a sight. A lamp-cabin attendant (whose sober disposition Alf was quick to establish) told the journalist that 'they were walking in companies of ten or twelve', so fearful were they of this silent figure who 'strutted about the roads' as though 'enveloped in a white sheet'. That it may have been a local joker abusing his bed-linen cannot, of course, be dismissed, but the purposes of any such lengthy deception – reports continued from February to April – would be difficult to fathom.

In May, the 'Nine Days Wonder' of the General Strike – where miners were branded as 'revolutionaries' intent (in the words of an infamous *Daily Mail* editorial of 3 May) on 'destroying the government and subverting the rights and liberties of the people' – took attention, and, in the politically Liberal but temperamentally Tory stronghold of Stirling, took sympathy away from the miners. George V's chiding 'Try living on their wages before you judge them' fell on the deaf ears of many of his faithful subjects. Perhaps local lack of sympathy is understandable, if not excusable: Stirling was dominated by small-scale family businesses, with most employment being in retail, domestic services and other non-industrial work. A further four-month stoppage followed, and the *Stirling Sentinel* bewailed 'Mad Britain!' and called the stoppage 'a disaster upon a disaster', hypocritically railing against the selfishness of the strikers at incurring a tally of £1,565 on the town for July's Poor Relief, alongside woeful articles about the miners' malnourished offspring and the County Medical Officer's opinion that one in four of their rented lodgings was 'unfit for human habitation'. For whatever reason, a mysterious *something* or *someone* frightening miners was not going to concern the majority of Stirling's citizens.

With the strike accounts of the 'Millhall Ghost', as it had now become known, the sightings did not cease, but, rather, moved into the heart of the town. A woman returning from visiting a family friend was alarmed by a still and silent 'white-clad figure' as she hurried home after midnight through the Ballengeich Cemetery. A lad was terrified by a similarly uncommunicative wraith in the Raploch. When a Castlehill woman fainted, following the frightful appearance of a blank-faced figure at her window, the mob mentality took over and about a hundred people armed with lanterns and cudgels made a furious search of the Old Town. Nothing was found. On each occasion, the supposed phantom was seen in those areas of the town worst affected by the deprivations the strikes had forced upon the struggling workers and their families – the filthy tumbledown hovels of Spittal Street, St Mary's Wynd and elsewhere – dives where all manner of dangers, real and imagined, lurked. With an estimated 290 people living per acre in Broad Street (the Burgh average was fourteen), it's easy to imagine how anxieties might manifest themselves during times of tension. Craig Mair, in *Stirling: The Royal Burgh*, quotes one local miner who wondered why the council couldn't 'knock down some of these old houses … and let the poorer class have a mouthful of fresh air and perhaps a little sunshine?' When the strike was broken, the ghost appeared once again – albeit briefly – on the summit of the Ballengeich, seeming to look down disparagingly on the defeated, dispirited miners as they returned to work. Alf was persuaded by the editor of the Labour newspaper, the *Daily Herald*, to spend an evening in the cemetery: 'it was a nice night' he reported. 'I spent four or five hours there but not a sound did I hear, except having a chat with the policeman on night duty.' Aware of recent frights, the constable had asked him to explain his presence in the graveyard. To the law-officer's surprise, the scribbler simply smiled that he was 'waiting for the Millhall Ghost'. It was never reported again.

Speculating on Alfred Reilly's commentary, R.J. Ritchie wondered, in 'A Chiel Haes Mind', if such 'ghosts' are a 'creation of our subconscious mind which intrude into our consciousness as an apparition'. If so, then the disappearance of this peculiarly political phantom may be put down to the environmental exorcism provided by the urban improvement programmes of the following quarter century. Though much diluted, the tale has not vanished along with the generation who first reported it. Tolbooth technician, James Wigglesworth, recalls trembling with terror, slumped in the back seat of his elderly aunt's car as they drove through modern Millhall during his youth in the 1970s, fearful of catching a glimpse of Reilly's favourite wraith.

Hearing of my interest in this particular phantom, I was sought out by a retired gentleman, Ken, who had been Head Porter of Stirling University's halls of residence during my undergraduacy. Working as a railway signalman in the 1950s and '60s, he had often cycled home along that same dark road at the end of his late-shift. 'There were no lights on the road, back then', he told me. He continued:

The light on my bike was powered by a wee dynamo, and started playing up, so I stopped to see what was the matter – and noticed what looked like wisps of light drifting across the road up ahead of me. I was straight back on my bike and pedalling hell-for-leather homeward before you could blink.

Ken confessed that he hadn't thought of the incident for nearly half a century, the memory awakened by my plea in the local press for information concerning this fickly fame-worthy phantom, but wonders if he may have encountered the 'Millhall Ghost'.

The overcrowded tenements of St Mary's Wynd, one of the haunts of the 1926 'Millhall Ghost'. (Picture reproduced by kind permission of the Smith Art Gallery & Museum)

Blind Alick

Any account of Stirling's kirkyards would be incomplete without some mention of our own 'manic street preacher', Alick Lyon. Blind Alick, as he was better known, was a familiar face in the Old Town taverns of the late eighteenth and early nineteenth centuries. According to legend, he came there not to share a draught with the worthies and wastrels, but to spread the word of God to those with half an ear – or half a mind – to hear. Blind since birth, Lyon had but one constant companion, his Bible, though he had no need of that Good Book. His memory of scripture never failed to impress even the dullest drunkards. They had no time for such saintly scribblings themselves, but found sport in offering whispered wagers to test the blind man's wits. One storm-lashed eve, as Alick preached and prattled on the evils of the demon drink, the barkeep sought a crueller entertainment. He wrenched the Bible from the preacher's breast and cast it out into the muck of the gutter. Then, jesting that his sport was too subtle for a sightless man to see, he hurled the preacher after it. The drinkers did nought to aid old Alick. They turned their eyes away, blind to his woes. None save the barkeep saw the bitter fire of righteous rage reflected in the old man's face as he raised his battered bones from the stinking mire and turned his sightless gaze upon the laughing bully. 'Let the wicked forsake his way', the old man growled, 'and the unrighteous man his thoughts: and let him return unto the Lord, and He will have mercy upon him.' Without another word he turned on his heel and – never missing a step – hastened into the darkness. He did not return. Word was that he had died soon after; his old bones were found, lonely and neglected, in his dusty rooms in Quality Street.

Months passed. One evening, their drinking done, the tardy tavern-dwellers set off across the Old Kirkyard to their homes beyond the Gowan Hill. As the Ladies' Hill loured before them, something caught their gaze, framed on its summit by the orb of the full moon – two figures, locked in some terrible conflict. The drunkards laughed and hurried on, eager to discover which of their cronies were contesting on the stony hillock – then stopped, their hearts skipping a beat as they saw the pair more clearly. The first they recognised in an instant – Blind Alick Lyon, risen from the grave, his Bible clutched, as ever, to his feeble frame. The other was a fiend born of nightmare – though each man present knew his name well enough – Lucifer, Beelzebub, the Morningstar; Satan himself in the form of a great beast. The preacher's milky eyes bulged as the creature grasped a calloused claw about his throat and squeezed the breath from him. Still he struggled on – wrestling, writhing, grabbling, grappling – begging that the Lord might send his servant strength to cast the demon out. Welling up his will, Alick arched his Bible high above his head, plunging it downward, deep into the beast's black heart. An ungodly wail cut through the night, a blinding blaze of hellfire bleached the hillside. The drunkards were left alone, trembling amid the tombstones. In the days to come each would sign The Pledge and foreswear the demon drink forevermore.

It is a fine story: a righteous rejoinder that we should never underestimate the wit or worth of the outcast and the underdog – and, of course, a suitable stern condemnation

of those that deal and delight in hard liquor. It was, unsurprisingly, a favourite temperance tale – and the very first Stirling ghost story I ever heard – from the elderly neighbour of a couple from whom I rented a room as an undergraduate in the town.

What is rare, in Stirling, is that it's a ghost story which features an identifiable historical figure – which, unfortunately, is its undoing. Alick (Alexander) Lyon had been a famous figure, and not just in the Burgh. The Boys Scrap Book of the American Sunday-School Union (1839) holds him up as an exemplar of 'faithful fortitude', noting his 'retentive memory, and the extreme acuteness of those senses on which the blind depend for compensating … for the loss of sight'. His knowledge of scripture was prodigious. Within his own lifetime, *The Penny Magazine* (#49, January 1833), published by the Society for the Diffusion of Useful Knowledge, gave an account of a gentleman who sought to test his memory. They asked him to recite the ninetieth verse of the seventh chapter of Numbers. 'You are fooling me sirs!' chided a canny Alick, 'There is no such verse – that chapter has only eighty-nine verses!'

The last of the great Victorians, Sir James Crichton-Brown, mentions his grandmother's recollection of that 'special gift of touch' by which Lyon was able to identify soldier from civilian by 'touching with his forefinger the coat of each that he passed' – but notes that the coarse wool of a guardsman's tunic might just be of a more telling texture than genteel and delicate civilian garb. He was a remarkable fellow, and one whose amazing abilities were almost certain to ensure his fame in the folk-record of the communities of the Castle Crag. What is rarely mentioned is that Alick was a beggar, who relied on such 'party-pieces' for his survival. *The Penny Magazine* expressed amazement that his memory had not only resisted the 'encroachments of old age' (he was seventy-three when he died) but also a force 'still more destructive to that faculty of the mind, the impairing effect of strong drink'. So Alick liked a tipple, after all: so much for temperance. His elevation from local oddity to fiery beast-wrangling preacher begins in earnest with the quite dreadful dedicatory doggerel of William Finlayson, in 1828, who composed a wearyingly lengthy first-person oration, wherein the (newly loquacious) beggar boasts:

'Choose death' – Blind Alick and the Green Lady move with the times. A promotional poster for the 1996 Stirling GhostWalk. (Image courtesy of Heritage Events Co.)

> Then from the slumbers of the tomb
> I shall awake and see
> Wonders to me unseen – unknown –
> All full disclosed to me …
>
> Though temporal blindness may enfold,
> And darkness dwell around,
> Yet doth thy powers all light behold,
> Through Faith's triumphant sound.

I am happy to report that Finlayson did not give up his day job. Confusion occurs through the existence of another 'Blind Alick', Alexander Macdonald, who was active during the same era. A far more fiery and contentious Clydeside character, Macdonald – dubbed the 'Glasgow Homer' – was a street vocalist and fiddler, famed for extemporising patriotic ballads, and taking pointed pot-shots at the powers-that-be. His orations were appropriately mythic, often giving grand account of the service of Scots regiments at Waterloo and elsewhere. Almost as legendary were the more domestic battles his politicking provoked.

Whatever the cause, each description of *our* Alick's famous faculties seems to have become more fantastic than the last. One account, describing Alick's muddled mind when his door-key was taken from him, becomes so exaggerated that it seems to be the key itself which mystically imbues him with his mythic memory. That an old blind beggar might simply be worried by the prospect of getting his key back from tricky strangers intent on testing him doesn't seem to have occurred to anyone. If the ghost

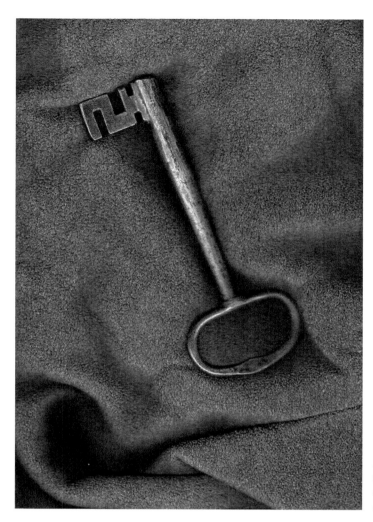

Blind Alick's key? An item from a Perthshire antiquary's collection. (David Kinnaird)

of Blind Alick ever appeared atop the Ladies' Hill, he certainly hasn't been seen for a long time – but that has not prevented him from enjoying an enduring fame not found by other colourful worthies of his era, like 'Bummin' Jamie', 'Humphie Geordie' and 'Cocky Riddell', or his ghost story becoming 'common knowledge' and a testament to the evolutionary nature of local legend.

Ill Met By Moonlight

One final tale before we depart the Old Kirkyard. Some years ago, I was called upon by a corporate event organiser to tell a number of Stirling's tales of terror to a group of businessmen banqueting within the walls of Stirling Castle. As was often the case with such functions, a surfeit of self-aggrandising speechifying caused events to overrun, and I didn't finish my final story until well after midnight.

The Holy Rude – a church and cemetery has stood on this site since the thirteenth century – has been a bloody battleground three times during its history. (David Kinnaird)

Living only a short distance from the fortress, I had got into costume and suitably macabre make-up at home. Garbed as David Seton, the feared seventeenth-century witchfinder – or 'common-pricker', as they were known north of the Border, on account of their favoured practice of thrusting a brazier-heated bodkin into the accused to test if their 'unnaturall fleshe' would bleed (which, of course, it didn't – the wound having been neatly cauterised) – I had walked briskly up the Castlehill to my place of work. I saw no reason, having now concluded my day's labours, not to return the same way – but chose to take a short-cut across the Valley and Holy Rude kirkyards. It was an appropriately dark and stormy night. I wrapped my cloak around me as protection against the bitter chill of the winter wind, and walked swiftly through the overgrown pathways of the necropolis. I hasten to add that I'm no 'whistler in the dark', easily affrighted by these gardens of the dead – if so then I'd have been in the wrong line of work these past twenty years – I was simply cold, tired and eager to wipe away my ghoulish greasepaint.

I was surprised, though, to see a figure standing in the shadows, beneath the heavy overhanging branches which shrouded the walkway near Mar's Wark. A strange hour, I thought, for someone to be lurking in that secluded spot. Then I smiled to myself: however odd the reasons for this stranger's presence, *he* wasn't dressed like an extra from a Roger Corman movie. I thought he must surely have heard my approach, my boots crunching on the path, and – being a civil chap – I nodded a polite 'Good evening!', and doffed my hat as I passed. He looked up, wide-eyed and trembling with terror as his gaze met mine, and let out a shriek the likes of which I've rarely heard in twenty years of professionally petrifying people – before tearing off, full-tilt, toward the graveyard gate. Not, I'm sorry to say, the first time that has happened: when you spend much of your working life clad as a corpse it's easy to forget just how such sights can startle strangers. I thought to follow after him, to apologise for causing such alarm, but held my ground – realising that the sight of a cloak-flapping Vincent Price wannabe chasing him between the moonlit mausoleums might do little to calm his nerves. Then I noticed that he had dropped something. Lots of little somethings, if truth be told: a handful of clear plastic bags containing peculiar pills and powders – vanishing quickly into the mud of the puddled pathway. *Ah!* Suddenly the stranger's presence in this lonely spot wasn't quite so odd.

Weeks later, enjoying a much needed coffee between shows at the Old Town Jail, I related this encounter to the community policeman, Colin MacGregor, who laughed out loud. That might explain something he had been wondering about for some time, he said. Though the kirkyard was the only public part of the Burgh not now covered by CCTV cameras, the local drug dealers were curiously reluctant to revel in its secluded safety from prying eyes. For some reason they'd got it into their heads that the place was haunted. I wonder why?

GhostWalking – author David Kinnaird has been entertaining audiences in Stirling's spectral heart for twenty years. (Photograph by Patricia Brannigan)

The Heading Hill

Gowan Hill

Continuing the course of the Back Walk from the kirkyards, walkers are led through the dense scrub and woodlands surrounding the steep volcanic mound of Stirling Castle to the Gowan Hill. Here, commanding suitably majestic views of the fortress behind and of the city below, and covered by a conical iron grille, can be found the beheading stone. This was the 'Heading Hill' – the crime of high treason for which the penalty of beheading was reserved, being suitably distanced from the more public and populous exhibitions of punishment at the Barras Yett. It was here, upon this weatherworn block, that Murdoch Stewart, Duke of Albany, his sons Walter and Alisdair, and his father-in-law, Donnchadh of Lennox, were beheaded on the orders of James I, on 24 May 1425. The monarch was clearly displeased by that Governor of Scotland's self-serving mismanagement of his kingdom during his own imprisonment by England's Edward IV (or angered by Stewart's refusal to pay the ransom which would have ensured his release years earlier). James's bride, Joan Beaufort, continued the family tradition in 1437 by despatching one of his murderers on the same spot, after a three-day carnival of wifely wrath involving crucifixion, scourging, branding, partial dismemberment and (finally, *mercifully*) beheading. The incident is recalled in an anonymous fifteenth-century toast:

> Robert Graham
> Who slew our King.
> God give him shame.

As such punishments became rare, the beheading stone was forgotten – it was not used in the despatch of the Radical weavers Baird and Hardie in 1820 – and was rediscovered in 1887, sunken into the earth by the Old Bridge, where it was being used as a chopping-block for de-horning sheep by a local butcher. It was rescued and restored to its place of honour by the Stirling Natural History & Archaeology Society the following year. Jacobite guns were foolishly placed here in January 1746, during Charles Edward Stuart's siege of the castle – only to be swiftly smashed by the artillery of the French Spur.

Curiously, the bloody history of the 'Heading Hill' does not appear to be reflected in the few tales of phantoms associated with 'The Gownie'. Thirdman, posting on the Ghost Finders Scotland website (www.ghostfinders.com.uk) relates an incident from his youth: 'I saw a woman at the beheading stone, a long time ago,' he writes. 'She came out of nowhere and stood next to me, looking straight at me. My instincts were telling me something wasn't right so I got out of there as fast as I could.'

An oft-reported local anecdote features not one but three female figures at this lonely spot, encountered by a jogger catching his breath on the bench facing out over the Forth Valley. Replying to Thirdman's comment, another forum member recounts

The beheading block upon which aristocratic traitors were executed, and the distant Wallace Monument. (David Kinnaird)

this familiar tale, reporting how the ladies allegedly appeared nearby the resting runner and 'wandered around the stone several times'; as he got up and resumed his exercise, he 'looked up and there was nobody to be seen'.

This was another familiar haunt, in decades past, of the Pink Lady and – I was informed by one enthusiastic Bridge of Allen lady, Miss Evelyn Brooks – of a *White* Lady. This, I was assured, was none other than the famous 'White Lady of Rownam Avenue', whose legend was popularised by the prolific Irish folklorist and ghost-hunter Elliott O'Donnell, in his entertaining anthology *Scottish Ghost Stories*. O'Donnell writes of 'a lady in white … whose death at a very early age had been hastened, if not entirely accounted for, by her husband's harsh treatment,' who appears wrapped in the white winding-sheet in which she was buried. The tale, apparently related to the author by a friend's acquaintance while visiting Edinburgh, tells of this man's earnest efforts, as a boy, to catch a glimpse of the famous phantom, by creeping onto the grounds of Rownam Manor House. The master of the house (the wraith's widower), 'Sir E.C.', was 'held in such universal awe and abhorrence that we used to fly at his approach, and never spoke of him amongst ourselves saving in such terms as "Auld

Dour Crab", or "The Laird Deil'". Concealing himself in the leafy gloom of the estate, the plucky lad – in an account which owes a great deal to the spirit of Wilkie Collins, if to no other – caught a glimpse of the wistful wraith, delighting in the 'dainty curves of her full red lips and the snowy whiteness of her perfect teeth. Nothing … on Earth or in Heaven could have been half so lovely.' But all, it seems, was not as it appeared. As the figure glided ever-closer, he spied:

> walking by her side, with one arm round her waist, his face and figure illuminated with the light from her body, was Sir E.C. But how changed! Gone were the deep black scowl, the savage tightening of the jaws, and the intensely disagreeable expression that had earned for him the nickname of The Laird Deil, and in their stead I saw love … nothing but blind, infatuated, soul-devouring love – love for which no words can find an adequate description.

Next morning he heard that 'Sir E.C.' had died, and realised that the White Lady had returned to accompany her misanthropic (but misunderstood) spouse from this world to the next. A fine tale, replete with the requisite tragic twist of which our Victorian forbears were so fond. Unfortunately, it is complete and utter twaddle. There is not now and never has been a 'Rownam Avenue' or 'Rownam Manor House' in (or near) Stirling – though that has not prevented the story's listing in an astonishing number of paranormal gazetteers and internet archives of 'true tales', which often repeat O'Donnell's chronicle word-for-word. In some respects this is oddly fitting, as for all his earnest enthusiasm, the 'Dean of Ghost-Hunters' was often less than diligent in testing the veracity of his sources. James Robertson, in his own (rather more meticulously researched) *Scottish Ghost Stories*, comments that, for O'Donnell,

> the most effective story-telling style was to create a kind of Chinese puzzle whereby one narrator introduced another who might introduce another, and so forth, hustling the reader with confidence and gusto from marvel to marvel, giving him no time for reflection.

That certainly sounds like the internet to me. I include the 'famous' tale of the White Lady here merely because so many people – assuming it to be true, on account of the late Mr O'Donnell's reputation – have suggested that I must. At least one vague report of a white figure was reported here in the 1920s, but this appears to be a rogue visitation by Alf Reilly's wandering 'Millhall Ghost' – which may account for Miss Brooks' grafting O'Donnell's ghoul onto the spot.

four

Stirling Castle

'Stirling, like a huge brooch, clasps Highlands and Lowlands together.'
Alexander Smith

And laws for Scotland's weal ordain'd;
But now unroof'd their palace stands,
Their sceptre's sway'd by other hands;
The injured Stuart line is gone,
A race outlandish fills their throne;
An idiot race, to honour lost;
Who know them best despise them most.
Robert Burns, 'Lines on Stirling' (1787)

Two years after scratching these lines at King Street's Golden Lion Hotel, Burns complained – as he applied for a position as an exciseman (tax collector) in service to that self-same 'idiot race' – that he was still being 'blamed and schooled for my inscription on a Stirling window'. Tactlessness aside, his ire was well earned. The old place had certainly seen better days. There is little archaeological proof that the Romans, Votadini, Picts or Northumbrians fortified this great rocky promontory, but it would be most surprising if they had not. Its strategic importance in Scotland's history cannot be overestimated. It has been besieged by Henry II, William the Lion, Edward I, Edward II, Robert Bruce, General Wade, Charles Edward Stuart, and many more besides.

A favoured royal seat since the time of Alexander I, it was home to the Stuart dynasty: the 'Key to Scotland' – dividing north from south, Highland from Lowland. Here, in 1291, the Scots nobility swore fealty to the invading English, and within sight of its walls Wallace enjoyed his famous victory at Stirling Bridge, in 1297, and Bruce sent that Auld Enemy 'homeward to think again', at Bannockburn, in 1314. Within James IV's imposing defensive Forework, his successors all made their mark – from the ornate splendour of James V's Palace to his grandson James VI's stunning refurbishments of the Chapel Royal and Great Hall. With the Act of Union, in 1603, whereby both king and court were rudely transported to London, Stirling fell from prominence. Jamie the Saxt became James the First, too. He claimed he would return to the ancient seat of his forefathers, but never did, and by the time of Burns' visit in

The Valley – executions, jousting, duelling, witch-burning and horse trading are all to have occurred here, in the shadow of Stirling Castle. (David Kinnaird)

1787, Stirling Castle was little more than a neglected garrison. *Sic transit Gloria Scotia.*

Derek Green of The Ghost Club of Great Britain, one of the few paranormal investigators permitted the opportunity to study the castle first-hand, comments that 'the classic "ghost" is simply a playback in time to a specific event which harboured a positive or negative emotion.' Given the turbulent history of this finest of Scots fortresses, it would be remarkable if events here had *not* made their mark.

The Highland Soldier

In 1992, knowing of my interest in matters anomalous, the late Chic Duthie – then head warden, and a fund of knowledge regarding mythic and historical lore relating to the castle – alerted me to an odd item on display in the Museum of the Argyll and Sutherland Highlanders. It was a photograph, taken around 1935 by an unnamed architect. The picture had shortly thereafter come into the possession of the photographer's friend, Lieutenant General Sir Humphrey Gale. It was a study of the Upper Close, the archway linking the grand sixteenth-century palace of James V with the Great Hall, and leading into the Upper Square – spoiled by what appeared to be the fleeting shadow of a kilted figure lumbering through the arch and into the courtyard above. This was most curious. The photographer told Sir Humphrey that he recalled the sentry who had greeted him at the Main Gate, but had been aware of no-one else nearby as he laboured behind his lens in the Lower Square. In daylight hours, the archway provided access between the soldiers' quarters and those of the staff sergeant. It was a busy thoroughfare – but the photographer had elected upon the early hours for his endeavour, specifically that he might avoid the interruptions that workaday soldierly life within that place would bring, and was sure he would have recalled any such intrusion.

The photograph passed into the hands of barrister Reggie Bell and thence to his cousin Reggie MacLeod, who presented it in trust to the castle's regimental museum

The castle's famous ghost photograph. (Reproduced with the kind permission of the Museum of the Argyll and Sutherland Highlanders)

some time before his death in 1992. The photograph proved popular with visitors, and has been available as a postcard image ever since. MacLeod, described by long-term friend and physiotherapist Margaret Measures as a 'level-headed man, not at all given to fantasy', was convinced that the photograph was more than just another couthy conversation piece. It does not appear to be a double exposure – if it were, then the fractional movement of the camera between shots would surely have resulted in tell-tale blurring of the surrounding stonework. That the image was taken on a fairly sophisticated camera is evidenced by the simple fact that there is no indication of the verticals converging (as would occur with more basic lenses), so the usual faults and foibles responsible for the creation of so many misleading 'spooky' images wouldn't immediately appear to apply. Fakery is always an option, of course – and the distinguished Sir Humphrey, the photograph's first *named* owner, was certainly known to possess a wicked sense of humour, on occasion – but if that were the case then the purposes of this deception are unclear, as the picture was not subject to public display or discussion until comparatively recently.

Martin Coventry, in *Haunted Castles & Houses of Scotland*, reports that two soldiers observed a kilted figure in unfamiliar uniform march along the battlements leading from the Douglas Gardens in 1952, vanishing where the walkway intersects with the Governor's Block – its course in line with that of the original defensive walkway. Guides joke that the ghostly Argyll may still be keeping watch, so frequent are the reports of visitors' encounters with a mysterious kilted character – often described as looking like a soldier or tour guide.

A typical account comes from Margot Obermeyer, a holidaymaker from Nebraska who visited the castle in 1998. She was angered when the uniformed 'guard' standing by an archway in the Lower Square ignored her repeated requests to be directed to the nearest bathroom, turned, and walked into the tunnelled entrance to the Lion's Den, the site of the former Royal Menagerie. 'It was just plain ignorant behaviour,' she said, 'so I decided I'd give him a piece of my mind.' She hurried after him, only to discover that the dingy corridor was completely empty. 'I can't have been more than a few feet behind him, but he was nowhere to be found.' Mrs Obermeyer was mildly alarmed by this occurrence – but was much relieved to find the washrooms she craved, at the far end of the passage, as she searched in vain for the vanished 'Kiltie'. The entrance in question, incidentally, would once have provided a short-cut to the canteen and soldiers' quarters — first ports-of-call for a weary squaddie finishing his watch. Having inadvertently alarmed many a skittish visitor while heading to-and-from performances in period costume — I once caused a woman to faint in the Old Kitchens when I stepped from an alcove grimly garbed as the sixteenth-century preacher John Knox — I am always wary of such accounts. More recently, a tourist was alarmed by an apparent power-cut while in the depths of the ruined Elphinstone Tower, and was grateful to the kilted gent who aided her ascent from its murky gloom into the bright light of day. As she turned to thank her helper — an actor, she imagined, from one of the performances which entertain tourists throughout the summer season — she found he had slipped away. She spoke to one of the guides at the gatehouse as she departed, asking him to be sure to let the thespian know she was most grateful for his kindness. The guide was a little taken aback — as no performers or costumed characters were present that day.

The Green Lady

The Argylls — Balaclava's infamous 'Thin Red Line' — have a centuries old association with Stirling Castle, extending beyond the recent amalgamation of Scottish soldiery into the Royal Regiment of Scotland in March 2006. Its regimental museum is still based within the King's Old Building in the Upper Square — a structure which, as John and Julia Keay rightly note in the *Collins Encyclopaedia of Scotland*, 'defies architectural interpretation'. Greatly remodelled in the Scots Baronial style by Robert William Billings following the devastation of a fire in the nineteenth century, this peculiar building incorporates the mediaeval royal apartments of James IV, completed around 1497, and at least one much older structure, built on a different alignment to both the King's Old Building and the sixteenth-century palace which succeeded it. Excavation of this latter site in 1998 uncovered numerous burials, leading to conjecture that this may have served as a royal chapel during the reign of James I, or earlier.

Performing in the neighbouring palace during the 1990s, I often encountered reports that cleaners working within the Argylls' chambers had heard heavy footsteps padding across the ceiling. Similar accounts had apparently been offered by soldiers stationed there in the 1940s and '50s. It would have been impossible — or at least exceedingly difficult — for anyone to walk steadily across that narrow, slatted roof. Intriguingly, there *had* been a sentry beat along just that area until Billings' brutal remodelling of 1855. According to tradition, a relief sentry ascended the (still extant) stairway to this narrow walkway sometime in the 1820s, only to discover his predecessor dead at his post, a look of terror on his face. He must, the story goes, have met the gaze of the Green Lady — for to do so is to invite death before the dawn.

If Auld Staney Breeks is the most notorious of the Old Town's apparitions, then the Green Lady is certainly its most celebrated. Yet for all her ubiquity and the fabled fatality of her encounters, there is very little consensus as to who, or what, she is.

I recently asked three guides within Stirling's Smith Art Gallery & Museum – local women, raised within streets of one another and more familiar than most with local lore – to tell me the tale of the town's most famous female phantom. Each told me a different story. According to one she was a bride who died of a broken heart when her betrothed perished during Edward I's gruelling four-month siege of Stirling, in 1304, and whose wraith walks woefully between the castle and the kirk. To another she is the unfortunate daughter of a castle governor who foolishly fell for a common guardsman, whose attentions (and life) were terminated by her furious parent, who imprisoned her within the Elphinstone Tower, lest her distress reveal his fatherly felony. From here she cast herself onto the ragged rocks below, ending her life. In the third's account she was a Highland servant girl who died saving her mistress – the equally ubiquitous Mary, Queen of Scots – from a burning bedchamber, during a fire in 1561. All origins, you may recall from the previous chapter, are also attributed to the graveyard's Pink Lady (also rumoured to be an occasional castle visitor).

There is absolutely nothing in the historical record to support the first tale – save that Longshanks' siege occurred, and that a church has stood on the site of the current (mostly fifteenth and sixteenth century) Holy Rude kirk since at least 1129. Proof of the second – the most popular version for a great many years, and recounted frequently by the likes of Drysdale, Fleming and, in the twentieth century, by Alfred Reilly, is equally elusive. The barely averted immolation of Mary – on 13 September 1561 – *is*, however, a matter of record.

According to the most popular version of the tale, Mary had in her service at that time a girl of good Highland stock, said – like many of our Celtic cousins – to possess the second sight, the ability to foresee the future. As they approached Stirling Castle, this girl was gripped by a terrible premonition that the queen would come to some calamitous end if she slept the night within those walls. She begged her monarch's indulgence, told her tale, and was relieved that her fears were not dismissed as girlish folly. Mary was fond of the girl, but was weary, and could not bring herself to turn away from the town simply to appease a young girl's fearful fancy. Still, she was mindful of an old prophesy that a queen would come to an untimely end in Stirling, and took precautions to ensure her safety. It was decided that the augur of woe – the Highland lass herself – should keep watch over her as she slept. Who better to keep her from harm than one who could see it coming? For long and weary hours the girl sat and fretted, her gaze never fleeting from her queen. She had lit a candle, and set that waxen taper by Mary's bedside, but found little warmth or comfort in its flickering flame. The drear darkness of the autumn night seemed unending. As minutes passed into hours and hours to a seeming eternity, the young seer began to doubt her own foretelling. What possible harm could await Mary in this place? Who would conspire against her here? The more convinced the lass became of her own error, the more leaden were her limbs, and the heavier her eyes. She closed them – just for a moment, no more than that – and fell, in that moment, into a fitful slumber. She can only have slept for moments, seconds perhaps – but started awake, spluttering, her eyes blinking in the sudden bitter brightness. The room was ablaze. The taper placed by her monarch's bedside had toppled, the flame quickly consuming the tapestries adorning her bedposts. The sheets and carpets quickly followed. She called to the queen, but could not rouse her from her rest. She called for aid, but the bitter pall of smoke had robbed her of her voice. Bravely she bundled the sleeping Mary in her arms and made toward the door, bracing herself against the pain as the flaming fibres flicked at her emerald gown, consuming her soft young flesh …

That a candle-flame set fire to the queen's bed-curtains is known from the Calendar of State Papers. One English statesman, Sir Thomas Randolph, a cynical commentator on the affairs of Mary's Court, made reference to the old prophesy that a queen would burn in Stirling – noting ruefully, as Lady Antonia Fraser reports in her biography of

James V's Palace, viewed from the Ladies' Hill. Mary, Queen of Scots was saved from a fiery end here in 1653. (Patricia Brannigan)

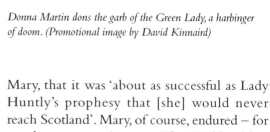

Donna Martin dons the garb of the Green Lady, a harbinger of doom. (Promotional image by David Kinnaird)

Mary, that it was 'about as successful as Lady Huntly's prophesy that [she] would never reach Scotland'. Mary, of course, endured – for another twenty-six years. The Highland lass – whose intervention (and existence) is not chronicled – apparently did not. In penance for her folly – accidentally creating the catastrophe which threatened the queen and (ironically) robbed her of her own life – her spirit is said to appear as a harbinger of doom for those that bide within the fortress.

Alfred G. Reilly offers an intriguing addendum to this tale. In 1929, Alf – reported in R.J. Ritchie's biographical tribute, 'A Chiel Haes Mind' – was called upon to visit a young Argyll 'absolutely frightened out of his wits', being cared for in the military hospital which was then occupying the seventeenth-century Argyll's Ludging in Castle Wynd (*see* Chapter 5). The young man, 'a Yorkshire laddie who knew nothing about ghosts there', reported a disturbing encounter on the stairwell which once led to the sentry-beat above the King's Old Building. 'I was going up there – they're narrow stairs, you know – and when I looked up there was a beautiful lady all in green coming down. I pressed myself against the wall to give her room to get past.' Alf enquired of the young serviceman what happened next. 'She walked right through me, and the next thing I'd collapsed.' Reilly, as cynical and world-weary a regional hack as one can readily imagine, shared the opinion of the attending medical officer and the lad's regimental sergeant major, Andrew Hutton, that he was utterly sincere: 'I believed the laddie. He was so frightened. He couldn't be kidding me. He was narrating just what happened.' The Green Lady? If so then it is fortunate that the anxious squaddie doesn't seem to have caught her eye.

'A Douglas by his Sovereign bled'

One current guide tells of a security guard who, patrolling the castle at night, chided a colleague for neglecting to lock the heavy iron gate allowing access from the Upper Square into the Douglas Garden. His compatriot took umbrage at this complaint, insisting that the entrance had been checked and secured mere minutes before. Thinking no more of the matter, the officer turned his own heavy key in the lock, shook the gate to ensure that is was closed tight, and went about his business – only to find it swinging on its hinges, once more, when he made his next inspection.

I recall hearing similar tales when I first worked within the castle twenty years ago, and visitors have often commented on a peculiar atmosphere in this quiet, verdant nook between the old apartments and Chapel Royal. Its calm façade belies the dark history from which it takes its name – the brutal murder of William, 8th Earl of Douglas, within the adjacent King's Old Building, on 22 February 1452.

Relations between the houses of Stuart and Douglas had long been strained. Archibald, the 5th Earl, had served as regent to the young King James II until his death in 1439, and his heir was proving to be a headstrong and troublesome youth. Popular, too. Aged only fifteen, he had haughtily refused a summons to take his place at the Scots Parliament, and commanded a fighting force the equal of any in the land. On 28 November 1440 the boy was summoned, along with his younger brother, to dine with the nine-year-old monarch at Edinburgh Castle – the invitation issued by Sir William Crichton and the castle governor, Sir Alexander Lindsay, both wary of the earl's growing ambition and influence on the young king. Concluding their repast, Crichton placed a black bull's head before the guests – a traditional emblem of impending doom. Before the young warrior could react, the governor's guards were upon him. The tearful James had to be restrained as his guests were brutally beaten, then dragged to the capital's Castlehill where they were beheaded as traitors to his Crown.

Reaching the age of majority, James seemingly sought to atone for the cruel injustice done in his name: Crichton and Livingstone were disgraced, William reclaimed (by marriage) his lordships of Bothwell, Whigtown and Galloway, and the Douglas name was once more honoured at Court. Yet, for all the formal façade of grace and favour, old resentments were never far from the surface. While William paid pilgrimage to Rome, James' men raided his lands, and Douglas fell in league with the traitorous Alexander, 'The Tiger', Earl of Crawford. As tensions grew, William was invited to sup with the

Stirling Castle, viewed from the Old Kirkyard. (Patricia Brannigan)

Some claim that the blackening of stones on the Holy Rude's bell-tower was caused by the blaze started by those avenging William Douglas's murder. (David Kinnaird)

king in his private rooms at Stirling Castle, that they might resolve their differences. Though understandably wary, given his kinsmen's cruel treatment at the 'Black Dinnour' twelve years before, William accepted – under Royal Licence of Safe-Conduct. James begged and pleaded with his former friend to abandon his treacherous alliances, and, when he refused, fell into a fury, murdering him with his own hands – stabbing him twenty-six times before hurling his corpse out of the window into the garden below, which now bears his name: 'A Douglas by his Sovereign bled' (Sir Walter Scott, 'The Lady of the Lake', 1810). The king's choice of defenestration over diplomacy was typical of his temperament. Known as 'Fiery Face' on account of his possession of a conspicuous vermilion birthmark, his petulance in perturbation was famously fervid.

If the irksome irritation of security guards is some peculiar revenant of revenge enacted by the earl's unquiet spirit, then he need not have bothered: an exploding cannon (his own) terminated the intemperate monarch's existence during his siege of Roxburgh Castle, on 3 August 1460. This incident is described by Robert Lindsay of Pitscottie in his *Historie and Chronicles of Scotland: 1436–1565* – 'his thigh-bone was dug into two with a piece of misframed gun that broke in shooting, by which he was stricken to the ground and died hastily' – and his kin enjoyed their own fiery revenge on James, and on the Royal Burgh, through their retaliatory raids of 1452 and 1455:

Other Encounters

Chic Duthie, interviewed by Steve McGrail for a 1996 *Fortean Times* feature on ghost photographs, was asked his thoughts on the many alleged strange encounters and anomalies reported within the castle walls. His response was guarded:

> I've never seen anything, but a few years back, when I was locking up one evening and was climbing the stair to the Great Hall, I felt a hand on my shoulder. I wasn't frightened, but when I turned around there was no-one there.

Historic Scotland's renovation and refurbishment of the castle is a constant process, requiring the diligence and dedication of dozens of highly-trained craftsmen. One young workman – another 'Yorkshire laddie', oddly enough – was labouring well into the summer night in the Great Square, replacing and refitting cobbles near the entrance to the Argyll's Museum. It was mid-evening, long after the building was closed to the public, and he was surprised to see someone lurking in the entrance. He called out, and the figure, wrapped in a full-length black coat or robe – hardly suited even to the Scottish summer weather – turned towards him. Beneath what appeared to be a hood or cowl, he could see no face. Leaving his tools, he spun on his heels, and ran. He did not return. A typically gothic ghost encounter, though it is perhaps worth noting that this visitation, according to the accounts of the incident related to me by members of the restoration team, was in the area where the remains of the supposed medieval royal chapel would soon be discovered – a chapel founded and served by Dominicans: Blackfriars, famed for their distinctive dark, hooded garb.

The Ghost Club

Founded in 1862, The Ghost Club is probably the world's oldest association dedicated to the study of alleged paranormal phenomena, and has counted amongst its membership such luminaries as Charles Dickens, Sherlock Holmes creator Sir Arthur Conan Doyle, poet W.B. Yeats, and a host of scientists, clergy, sceptics and enthusiasts, as well as those who claim mediumistic ability. The approach of its modern membership is rather more intensively interrogative than that of the excitable 'spiritist', whose dramatic demonstrations of psychic ability were greeted with barely disguised befuddlement at a meeting of local laity at the Holy Rude, in 1926. This led one disdainful kirk-wife to conclude that spiritualism was 'best left alone' (*Stirling Sentinel*, 23 February 1926).

Veteran investigator Tony Cornell, and psychic Glyn Edwards, had visited the site in March 1992 as part of a *Sightings* television feature on what it melodramatically (and inaccurately) dubbed 'Scotland's House of Horrors'. However, The Ghost Club's investigation, on Sunday, 2 March 2008 – conducted with the kind permission of the castle's custodians, Historic Scotland – was the first detailed paranormal investigation to occur within its walls. I am most grateful to The Ghost Club's investigations organiser, Derek Green, who co-ordinated this venture, and to Willie McEwan, Stirling Castle Visitor Services Manager, for allowing me the opportunity to read the extensive report compiled from the investigators' notes – on the strict understanding that Historic Scotland cannot be seen to endorse what are, after all, entirely speculative findings. During the course of the evening, two teams of investigators visited a number of locations within the castle, independently recording any spiritual impressions they felt to be present, along with audio recordings, and electromagnetic and thermostatic readings, then compared and collated their results. Accompanying The Ghost Club members on their vigil were Frank Shields and Brian Gibson, experienced castle guides with an extensive knowledge of the fortress, providing factual, historic counterpoint to the group's observations.

Unsurprisingly, given its long-standing martial associations, many of the ghosts and spirits sensed by the investigators were soldiers. Numerous names – 'Duff', 'Andrew

MacGregor' and 'Thompson' amongst them – presented themselves to one group gathered in the King's Guard Hall, like players in a spiritual tableau. The latter was a sorry figure, brought before a larger assembly of his peers with his hands tied securely by his side, perhaps awaiting execution, or a firing squad. Mr Green sensed this group to date to the early 1900s (though I have thus far been unable to locate an account in the historic record of specific events appropriate to the personnel described).

In the Great Hall, Chris De Rosa was surprised when the image of a large sailing ship entered his mind – apparently wholly unaware that food and festivities for the baptismal celebration of Prince Henry, the first-born son of James VI, were presented from the replica of such a vessel in that very chamber, in 1594. An illustration of the same can be found in the castle's lavishly illustrated guidebook, but investigation organiser Derek Green is adamant that neither Chris nor any other member of the team had any knowledge of this publication: 'After the investigation I purchased a guidebook and one for Chris. We were very pleasantly surprised indeed.'

In the castle kitchens, both teams sensed a timid young woman in her twenties, the name 'Elizabeth' being noted, separately, by both groups. Another spirit, a 'male energy', was also apparent: 'John' or 'Jack' – a more forceful and controlling figure, possibly responsible for the girl's anxiety. Other spirits were reported here, amongst them an old woman with a bad back, and – again appearing in the reports of both teams – a small child, wary of being caught or chastised. Marco Piva spoke of his left leg being warm, as though the infant – the name 'Edward' was offered by one team – was cowering at his knee. All in all, a scene of dominance and servility of the sort featured in many a period drama, and entirely appropriate to the atmospheric medieval kitchen tableau surrounding the group – replete with props and costumed mannequins. The oppressive 'male energy' was not, it seems, amenable to investigation. The response to attempts to communicate with the other spirits was a surly psychic 'Don't hold your breath!'

The castle's defences loom over a secluded nook of the graveyard. (David Kinnaird)

Another masculine essence was noted on the upper level of the Elphinstone Tower. The structure – which has been a 'tower' in name only since 1689, when it was reduced to a stump in order to make way for an artillery battery – has a long association with uncanny sensations. When I first worked at the castle, tales of guard-dogs whimpering at the prospect of approaching the tower entrance were rife – though no-one ever seemed to have met the security guard who allegedly reported this curious canine cowardice. It is important to note at this point that none of the investigators involved had the same degree of knowledge of the site which undoubtedly influences and informs my own interpretation of their findings. Derek Green notes that 'a lot of info was kept back from the team, and many of them were from down south. Most of [them] knew nothing about the castle.'

Here investigator Joan Green sensed the name 'Lachie' or 'Lachlan' and noted an inexplicably spicy odour. Another member of the team became aware of a man standing by the wall, facing the door on the lower floor, and had the odd impression that this figure had emerged out of the wall itself. Guide Frank Shields confirmed that a doorway *had* once existed in that very spot. Another psychic, Lynn Roberson, sensed that this had been the location for fearful, furtive meetings and the exchange of secrets, or that weapons might have been stored or concealed here, and a name – 'Gordon Stoddard' – seemed to suggest itself. Part of another team, inspecting the same area later in the evening, Chris De Rosa also felt that the tower might have been used for the storage of munitions. Stephanie MacDonald reported another 'male energy' – and the name 'Duncan' came to mind. Her descriptions were most vivid. She described 'Duncan' as wearing woollen trousers and a short dark jacket: a simple uniform. His hair was tied back and he knelt by the window, his rifle – a musket – at the ready, mindful, she was sure, of hidden dangers outside the castle walls. She felt certain that he was from the mid-1700s.

Some of these general impressions can be easily supported by the historical record. The tower was, at various points during its history, used as a store for gunpowder and munitions, officers' quarters, and – most notably during the Cromwellian and Jacobite sieges of 1651 and 1746 – as a look-out post. 'Duncan's dark woollen garb sounds not unlike an artillery pelisse of the era. While it is interesting – possibly even significant – that two sets of investigators report similar details, it may be hasty to read too much into some of these statements. The Elphinstone Tower did, after all, serve as a defensive structure for much of its history – easily implied by its design and location within the fortress – and even the most rudimentary knowledge of the history of Britain during the eighteenth century might subtly and subconsciously suggest associations and significances into otherwise mundane observations. It is, after all, the nature of the human mind to order and to rationalise random events and sensations.

More intriguing were the apparently random impressions which did *not* tally with obvious historical or cultural background: Kay Robertson sensed a woman's voice saying, '*Se e dos da e dos*' – a phrase which defied her understanding (a misheard snippet of Spanish or Portuguese, perhaps – '*dos dedos*' means 'two fingers', for example, though *that* would not be a particularly pleasant greeting from the Great Beyond). Joan Green's comment regarding a 'spicy' smell is interesting, as the presence of a kitchen in this

unlikely nook is not something which would immediately occur to even historically knowledgeable observers – though one *had* once been located there.

The scientific data recorded during the investigation – and *not* prone to quite the same subconscious susceptibilities as flesh and blood – is worth considering. Scanning the tower's lower floor with a thermal imager, team-member Dave Alderton noted what appeared to be a band of heat emanating from a particular point on the stone wall. Residual heat from the day's sunlight on the old bricks? A possibility, certainly – but would the warmth of a not particularly radiant Scottish spring sun be sufficient to leave such a localised impression so long into the evening? Monica Tandy recorded an inexplicable three-second blip on her EMF Meter and noted a brief drop in temperature.

Tony Cornell's 1992 inspection of the site also yielded some curious readings. 'Is [a ghost] in the mind of the person, or is it a real physical object?' Said Cornell, sensibly combating the horrific hyperbole of *Sightings'* Stirling show: 'We record any changes in the physical environment. Sound, sight, heat, geo-magnetic changes – any form of electrical change – because we don't know what makes these things occur.' Cornell left an infra-red camera and a standard video camera in the tower overnight. Next day, the visual record was disappointingly uneventful, but the audio portion of the recording contained what the programme's presenter dramatically described as 'moaning and screaming among the electronic static' ('heavy breathing' might be nearer the mark). For the veteran investigator, this data proved nothing other than that he could not immediately explain the oddity. He was wise to feel this way.

Guide Sandy Easson tells of being alarmed by similar sounds when he first visited the tower, much to the amusement of the more experienced staff member accompanying him. 'You heard something?' asked his stony-faced companion. Sandy nodded. His workmate laughed – and explained that the growling and wheezing seem to be distant echoes not of the dead, but of assistants chatting in the bookshop above. Gutters and long-forgotten air-vents have often confounded even the most earnest investigator.

In the King's Presence Chamber of the royal apartments, Soraya Badar's EMF Meter showed a sudden spike of activity, not explicable by any obvious environmental or electronic factors. This reading was accompanied by feelings of disquiet in other members of her party. Marco's camera became temperamental – switching itself on and off seemingly at random during his group's vigil in the Great Hall. Much of the electronics employed in the evening manifested similar problems. Conclusive of anomalous activity? By no means – but sufficient, surely, to give pause for thought. It is reassuring to discover that even those who seek to unravel such mysteries as these can be unsettled by them. One investigator, standing by the tower entrance towards the end of the vigil, thought she sensed a dark figure approach her. Her response was described as the 'Heebie-jeebies!'

Looking at The Ghost Club reports, the reader is immediately struck by two things: the earnest conviction of the participants and the degree to which the veracity of their impressions and observations is determined by individual perceptions. Does the spirit of a Highland soldier, possessed of enduring personality and intelligence, still walk these cobbled causeways? Has the ghost of a girl in green somehow ingrained itself upon the place through some event in her traumatic past? Are such sightings or sensations the result of suggestion, misperception or genuine spiritual energies? The individual must, as ever, make up their own mind. Whatever the truth of each tale may be, it is difficult to argue with Mr Green's assertion that the castle 'retains a lot of energy from its vibrant past'. The old place certainly has atmosphere.

five

Whines and Spirits

'Empty barrels mak the maist noise' (Trad.)

A Provostorial Poltergeist?

Darnley's Coffee House, Bow Street

That 16-18 Bow Street, better known to locals as 'Darnley's House', has survived into the twenty-first century owes much to the power of myth. The building narrowly escaped demolition during the urban renewals of the 1950s. It is easy to deride these clearances as little more than a shameful campaign of municipal vandalism, but by the middle of the twentieth century the overcrowding and poor sanitation which afflicted so much of the Old Town had taken its toll. Repair and renovation of this astonishing array of ramshackle Renaissance and Reformation dwellings was rejected, and residents found themselves relocated to new estates on the outskirts of town as bulldozers laid waste to the historic heart of the Burgh. A local medium suggested to me, as I began research for this volume, that the decimation of so many original properties at the heart of the town might account for the scarcity of spirits reported in the surrounding streets in recent years. 'Darnley's House' survived, largely due to the earnest

'Darnley's House' – a former tavern plagued by poltergeists. (David Kinnaird)

efforts of the Thistle Trust, founded in 1928 to rescue important properties from the wrecking-ball of modernity. A pair of captured Napoleonic cannonade facing its gated entrance from Broad Street seem to offer a knowing reminder that the old building survived by the skin of its teeth.

This seventeenth-century building has absolutely no direct connection to Lord Henry Darnley, second husband of Mary, Queen of Scots – though it is almost certainly belief in that association which encouraged the Trust to preserve it. The current building dates from at least half a century after poor Henry's explosive end – he was blown up by assassins at Kirk o' Field, on 10 February 1567 – though the land on which it sits *was* once part of the estate of John Erskine, Earl of Mar, guardian to Henry's son, King James VI (I). Upper chambers are reputed to have served as a nursery for James's own ill-starred heir, Prince Henry. They clearly didn't. Darnley was, however, rumoured to have frequented an inn (and brothel) which once occupied a site at the rear of the building which now bears his name – possibly the predecessor of the once-imposing Moir of Leckie's House, constructed by local burgess David Moir around 1659. In subsequent decades it saw service as a dairy, a baker's shop, a carpet-maker's workshop and a Tourist Information Centre. (Incidentally, staff at the town's current Dumbarton Road TIC report occasional rumblings and phantom footfalls in their empty upstairs offices during the winter months.) Its low, arched roofs currently provide accommodation for the Darnley Coffee House, and create a quaint and cosy atmosphere, as far from the archetypal image of the haunted house as one can imagine. That said, it has been host to all manner of peculiar happenings.

Current proprietor Niall Pleace confesses that such oddities have become part of his day-to-day life. Doors slam without cause or warning; pots and pans are spontaneously shunted from shelves and hooks; ingredients spill onto counters. Nothing *too* remarkable. Nothing, certainly, that couldn't be explained by careless stacking or, as Niall put it, 'shoogly hooks'. Some occurrences, though, are more resistant to easy rationalisations. One staff member is constantly frustrated that chairs, neatly regimented under dining tables at the end of each working day, are often found pulled out, or shoved tightly into out of the way nooks and crannies the next morning. In 1997, Pleace's father witnessed an unattended coffee-pot violently lurch from its stand in the empty kitchen area, shattering on the tiled floor. Niall had a similar experience more recently, when a half-full hexagonal glass of water was inexplicably observed to tilt sharply on its side on the perfectly flat and otherwise uncluttered kitchen counter, rather in defiance of the laws of physics. Only last year a white-faced customer confided that he was more than a little worried when he felt a firm hand suddenly squeeze his shoulder as he performed his ablutions in the patrons' tiny toilet cubicle (an alarming encounter on many levels).

An assistant at the nearby corner shop, Broad Street Stores, claims to have seen a mysterious face fearfully glowering from the gloom of its arched entrance in the dead of night. Customers occasionally comment on sudden drops of temperature in the smaller of the site's two dining areas. Interestingly, this curious chill is most common adjacent to a 6ft-square walled area next to the original stairwell, linking the old stables with the inn on the floor above (now converted into modern flats – and

Broad Street in 1938. Only a handful of these ancient tenements survived the urban redevelopments of the 1950s. (Picture reproduced by kind permission of the Smith Art Gallery & Museum)

The Bow Street dairy – 26 Bow Street in 1938. (Picture reproduced by kind permission of the Smith Art Gallery & Museum)

blocked off). This appears to be partly hollow. 'I'd love to take a sledgehammer and see what's in there!' says Niall. A walled-up chamber, perhaps? A hidden entrance to the long-vanished tavern cellars, or to one of the many secret tunnels reputed to link major Stirling landmarks with the royal apartments in Stirling Castle? We may never know. Propriety – and the coffee shop's listed building status – has stilled Mr Pleace's eager hand.

Spilled drinks, overturned chairs and occasional unsettling bathroom encounters might be surprising in the cosy confines of a modern coffee house, but – as any pub landlord can testily testify – are oddly appropriate to another role the building once played in the life of the Old Town. The Darnley occupies the arched and gated stables of what was once Jonet Kilbowie's Tavern, a favourite seventeenth-century haunt of local bailies (magistrates and councillors) whose boisterous behaviour and fondness for spirits (of the alcoholic variety) was legendary. The bailies, reported by J.S. Fleming in *The Old Ludgings of Stirling*, marked the Burgh's surrender to General Monck, in August 1651, by running up an astonishing bar-tab of £10 11s 4d. Could it be that this spirit of riotous assembly has endured to the present day? A noted TV psychic visited the Darnley Coffee House in 2006, and reported that a malign presence was in residence. One of the belligerent bailies, perhaps – or the provost himself? Having finally been persuaded (after much prompting) to settle their bar-bill with Mistress Kilbowie, they *fined* the biddie – for selling over-priced beer.

A Puzzling Photograph

Nicky-Tam's Bar & Bothy, Baker Street

The disruption of renovations may have resulted in the haunting of another local hostelry. Moving southward from 'Darnley's House' in Bow Street, towards the modern town centre, we find Baker Street. If Broad Street was the administrative heart of the Old Town, then this was its major mercantile artery, carrying trade – and the accumulated muck and mire of the market district – toward the River Forth and the Burgh's once thriving port. The Ordnance Survey map of Stirling for 1858 shows this busy thoroughfare as a mass of banks, businesses and taverns, linked by a spidery sprawl of interconnecting wynds and alleyways – very few of which would survive the following century.

Nicky-Tam's Bar & Bothy, Baker Street. (David Kinnaird)

Originally built as a bank in 1704, 29 Baker Street – known better for more than two centuries as the Caledonia Vaults – had found new service as a tavern within three decades of its original construction, in which capacity it continued until the end of the twentieth century. Andrea Lindsay and her husband Chris took over this architecturally undistinguished and much-altered property – whose principal claim to fame was its status as one of Scotland's few remaining Free Houses – in 1999. Run down and much neglected, the titular vaults long since filled in with earth and rubble, they decided that major refurbishment of the premises was in order. Chris, a skilled joiner, supervised efforts to strip away the accumulated paint and plasterwork of generations. He was pleased by the quick progress being made. When restorations moved upstairs he was less content.

Stripping away the degraded wall-sheeting in an alcove of what is now the function room, Chris made a most unexpected discovery – a large framed photograph of a stern and serious late-Victorian gentleman in what appears to be a clerical collar. The picture is currently displayed behind the bar. The former owners were unable to identify him, and the only clue to his identity is the name 'R. W. Campbell' scrawled on the back of the photograph, though as Brian Allan – who visited the site several times between 1999 and 2002 on behalf of Strange Phenomena Investigations – rightly observes, this is as likely the name of the photographer or commissioning customer as the sitter. No clergyman or town-officer (whose ceremonial garb might easily be mistaken for that of a cleric) of that name can be found in parish records.

Interestingly, the distinguished photographer James 'Jeems' Rae may have served briefly as landlord of the Caledonia Vaults in the late 1880s, but any connection he might have to the photograph or its subject are (as yet) unclear. Could the walled-up

area once have been a darkroom? A regular at the pub, a gentleman named Blueitt, claimed the photograph was a representation of his grandfather, who ran a butcher's shop in the vennel behind the bar. That shop certainly existed in the early years of the last century, but why a butcher should be in clerical garb remains a mystery: none of his kin (locally, at least) are known to have held ecclesiastical or municipal office. Whatever its origins, or the reasons for its curious concealment, the discovery of this image seems to have served as the catalyst for a whole host of anomalous occurrences.

The picture discovered walled up in a hidden room. (Photographed with the kind permission of Nicky-Tam's Bar & Bothy)

According to one tabloid, reporting the case shortly after the rebranded Nicky-Tam's Bar & Bothy first opened its doors in 1999, plumber Pete Richardson refused to work at night 'without a babysitter' after observing a shadowy figure walk toward him across the bar. Similar shadows were glimpsed by both licensees and customers near the main entrance; muttering was heard from a sealed cupboard-space in what is now the gents' toilet; Andrea's mother reported the unnerving experience of someone walking through her as she helped with work in the upstairs rooms; and the landlady herself observed luminous orbs emerging from a bricked-up fireplace after she had locked up one night; electrical equipment became inexplicably temperamental and compressed gas supplies to the beer pumps would shut off unexpectedly. For all the disruption, though, Andrea – hitherto a firm sceptic where supernatural matters were concerned – seemed sure that whatever spirits may be present approved of the couple's improvements to the premises.

She may have spoken too soon. Around 4 a.m. one morning in the spring of 2000, Chris – sleeping soundly in the newly-refurbished flat above the tavern – was startled into consciousness by the sensation of being throttled. He quickly calmed, reassuring himself that this was no more than a nightmare – but woke again with the same choking sensation of fingers tight about his throat a few nights later, *again* around 4 a.m. This was to become a regular occurrence. Andrea woke to the sound of scratching and rattling from the flat's kitchen. Thinking that her dog, Patsy, was playfully rummaging in the waste-bin, she called to it – and was surprised when the dutiful hound's quizzical gaze met her from its basket at the foot of the bed.

A later incident was the cause of much greater concern. Again Andrea woke around 4 a.m. to sounds within the flat – footsteps, this time, climbing the uncarpeted stairs

Baker Street and the Caledonia Vaults (fifth building from the left) in 1890. (Picture reproduced by kind permission of the Smith Art Gallery & Museum)

outside. She heard the creak and click of the flat's front door opening and closing. Chris was sleeping soundly beside her so she was understandably anxious as to the identity and intent of her uninvited guest as the steady footfalls grew louder, moving closer – through the hallway, and suddenly stopping by the bedroom entrance. Though she could see no-one in the shadows beyond the open doorway, she nervously held her breath, certain that someone was watching her. After a few more anxious moments, the footsteps returned the way they came, and the apartment was silent once more. Her head spinning, Andrea woke Chris, insisting that he inspect every nook and cranny in the place for some sign of their visitor. The door was locked, and nothing was out of place.

Brian Allan was accompanied on his various visits to Nicky-Tam's by mediums Anne-Marie Sneddon and Jim Lochhead, who had visited Argyll's Ludging with him the previous year. They were of the opinion that *several* spirits were present. On their first inspection, in March 1999, Jim reported two working men – from the 1870s he thought – contentedly watching proceedings from the snug adjacent to the cellar door, and commented that these spirits imbued the area with a very positive atmosphere. It felt 'lucky'. Anne-Marie sensed a third, more sombre entity of more recent vintage by the cellar door – a hostile presence, she believed – connected in some way to a murder she was sure had been committed in the bar in the 1920s. The wary spirit of a child – a boy of around ten years of age – was noted in the arched, claustrophobic cellar to the rear of the property. Allan's report on his investigation notes Sneddon's opinion that 'the child hiding in the cellar and the embittered, hostile presence in the bar were one and the same'. The boy, she felt, was the murder victim 'grown to adulthood and seeking revenge'.

Unfortunately, public records offer no support here. A barmaid was murdered in Baker Street, but in the nearby (and long-vanished) Star Bar, not the Caledonia Vaults – and in 1907. The nearest recorded homicide – historically and geographically – is that of four-year-old Nessie Reid, molested and strangled in a back-garden on the other side of Baker Street in March 1925, most probably by itinerant basket-maker Anthony 'Noble Dan' Bickerstaffe. She was 'done to death', as trial judge Lord Alness noted in his summation at Bickerstaffe's trial, 'with a ghoulish ferocity which was rare, if not unprecedented, at least in the annals of Scottish crime.' Poor Nessie's spirit *had* been reported seeking contact at séances – which the *Stirling Sentinel* noted (in September 1926) had become 'a popular pastime in the "Tap o' the Toon"' – bewailing the 'Not Proven' verdict awarded her murderer, whose subsequent criminal career seems to dispel any doubts as to his guilt. Climbing the stairs to the upper floors, Anne-Marie exclaimed, 'I just bumped into someone' – at precisely the spot where Andrea's mother had reported the same sensation so many months before.

Studying the mysterious photograph, Sneddon sensed a 'dark side' to the scowling subject, an association too, perhaps, with witchcraft. The image might have been sealed away, she speculated, by practitioners of sympathetic-magicks intent on gaining power over him. The medium also felt sure that the rooms in which the picture had been uncovered had once been used for ritual purposes. Ritual, of course, would hardly be an uncommon activity for a clergyman. More mundane alternatives are, of course, available. Brian Allan discovered that the rooms may have been used for Masonic gatherings in the mid-eighteenth century. Local rumour suggested that The Ancient Order of Foresters used the premises for the formation of Court 'Hope of Snowdon' 6987, in 1875, but this seems unlikely: Dr Roger Logan, director of the modern Foresters Heritage Trust, confirms that few of the Scots Forester Courts of the period met on licensed premises, and *none* in public houses.

The investigators returned again in May 2000, following the Lindsays' later and more alarming experiences. Allan noted 'a negative, dull feeling about the place' which had not been evident during earlier visits – a coldness, too, typical of classic 'hauntings' – though Brian is quick to note that this sensation 'appears to be subjective and therefore may be an aspect of "mind" or consciousness rather than a physical manifestation.' Anne-Marie Sneddon identified the night-visitor who had sought to choke Chris as the murder victim, previously sensed. The medium suggested a simple cleansing ritual – a quiet ceremony using nothing more exotic than a little salt and water – to allow the Lindsays peace of mind and permit their distressed and increasingly unruly house-guest passage to what Anne-Marie calls 'a place of healing'. Though lacking the melodrama of more media-friendly 'exorcisms', this ritual seems to have been effective: the young couple remained untroubled through the remainder of their tenancy. Current landlord, William Paterson, who took over the business from the Lindsays in 2007, reports only occasional minor disturbances – spontaneously spilled glasses and the like – though Nicky-Tam's Bar & Bothy still proudly proclaims itself to be 'The most haunted pub in Stirling'.

One last note, regarding the tavern's 'lucky corner' – the nook occupied by the two ghostly workers. Andrea often told the tale of a customer who gleefully gloated that he had five numbers up on his lottery card as he sat in the snug. On being jokingly invited to share his good fortune and buy a round of drinks, he suddenly vanished – never to be seen again. Some mysteries, it seems, are not so difficult to fathom.

Another Vigil

The Settle Inn, St Mary's Wynd

Another investigation occurred within Stirling's oldest pub, the Settle Inn – formerly the Red Lion – on 27 December 2008. A tavern since 1736, this narrow, early eighteenth-century structure, sweeping down into the street from Barn Road, is frequently mentioned as one of Stirling's 'most haunted' buildings. However, the barmaid I spoke to when I made a recent visit seemed blithely unaware of this reputation – save, she said, for the accounts of one regular drinker who claimed (half in jest) that the spirit of another 'drouthy neebor' could be sensed, from time to time, sitting on a beer-keg near the cellar entrance: an ideal libatory limbo for any dear-departed dipsomaniac. She's not alone; I drank here regularly as a student in the late 1980s, and was utterly oblivious to its ghostly associations.

A welcoming hostelry, and one of the rare few in the town that seems equally hospitable both to locals and to the itinerant undergraduate population, it has had its

The Settle Inn – oldest (and – allegedly – second most haunted) pub in Stirling. (Patricia Brannigan)

share of curious occurrences – though mostly of the overturned glasses, temperamental electrics variety, which seems par for the course in many public houses. Nothing as dramatic, certainly, as the events regularly reported at Nicky-Tam's, but sufficient over time to ensure its continued reputation as a haunted place. Local youth worker, street entertainer (British diabolo throwing champion 2001) and former barman at the Settle Inn, 'George the Juggler', lodged above the pub for some time and jokes that he 'got to know the ghosts very well'. The stairway to the first-floor apartment seemed to be particularly active. 'You always had the sense that someone was coming up the stairs, or was about to come into the flat,' says the entertainer, 'but if you looked, the stairway was empty.' George was also subject to the only frightening episode reported in the haunting of the pub. Returning from a juggling job in the north of Scotland at 3 a.m., he went straight to bed. Shortly afterwards he awoke with a jolt to find a dark, indistinct shape looming over him. He is adamant that this was no travel-weary nightmare evoked by exhaustion and the inauspicious nature of the date – Halloween.

Arriving at the inn at around 11 p.m., just as the pub was starting to quieten down after a busy night's business, the Spiritfinders team decided to begin its investigation on the upper floor, housing the owner's apartment. Almost immediately their medium, Michael, sensed the spirit of a small fair-haired boy, whom he identified as 'Matthew', and who appeared very protective of a second, female essence, a little girl. Moving into the dining area, the investigators placed EMF Meters on the table, 'asking out' for the spirits to affect the readings by increasing the strength of the signal. This they obligingly did. Michael became aware of another child – 'Amy' – who joined the others: a family group, he presumed, belonging to former occupants of the chambers.

The lack of period detail is infuriating here, as it makes any efforts of identification very difficult. Suffice to say, the names of children named 'Amy' or 'Matthew' do not appear on available nineteenth or twentieth-century census documents mentioning the property. The psychic requested that 'Amy' sit on the knee of another investigator, who was seated at the table, and again asked that she try to influence the EMF Meter (though how a frightened child, alive or dead, was expected to know how to achieve that end is not entirely clear). Steve began to feel very cold, a sensation which he associated with the presence of the spirit – though as Brian Allan sensibly observed with regard to similar experiences in Nicky-Tam's, this could simply have been an 'aspect of mind' – an expectation of suitably spectral coldness, as it were, subconsciously suggested by the medium's comments. The process was repeated: the spirit was this time requested to sit upon the knee of a female member of the team, who soon complained that she was 'freezing'. The EMF Meter seemed to spike, and the psychic reported that the ghostly children were agitated, frightened by the approach of an adult male presence from the stairs outside. This, Michael claimed, was their father. 'When they were in the physical body,' the account of the vigil on the Spiritfinders website states, if 'they heard him coming upstairs they would run and hide and be terrified of him.'

The investigators sought to photograph the area around which the spirits were said to be huddled, one claiming to capture images of two 'light shaded shapes' – or 'orbs' – which he believed were evidence of ethereal energies. A mirror was placed against the wall, and each member of the team took turns to sit before it and, staring into the reflection, bid the spirits show themselves in the glass. 'Some team members said they could see the face of the team member sitting in front of the mirror change shape,' the website says. Unsurprising. It is one of the certainties of perception that if one expects to see changes of this kind, one almost invariably will (a tendency known as *pareidolia*) – which is why this particular 'test' has been dismissed as little more than an amusing 'parlour trick' for decades. I was genuinely surprised to hear of it being used in any modern investigation.

Around 3 a.m., the pub long closed, the group moved downstairs, assembling in the low-roofed seating area at the back of the building. Here, Michael said, there was a 'vortex'. He 'asked out' again – calling for spirit contact – and soon reported that he could see 'soldiers lying on both sides of the room', as though the building were being used as sleeping quarters. While no specific, verifiable incident might explain this psychic impression, military use of this building was certainly a possibility – though not by forces stationed at Stirling Castle.

Many buildings in the town were appropriated by Jacobites during their siege, in 1746, and a two-gun rebel battery had been disastrously positioned on the nearby Gowan Hill. The huddle of houses on St Mary's Wynd would offer the nearest shelter from the garrison's defensive barrage. The Jacobites had been admitted to the town on 8 January, the council fearful of the damage to local life and property which the assault of an estimated 8 or 9,000 men – then ominously assembled outside the Burgh Gate – might incur. The castle's commander, Major-General Blakeney, saw this act of capitulation as cowardice, declaring 'as your provost and bailies think the town not worth their notice to take care of, neither can I. I shall take care of the castle' – and withdrew with the militia, and as many guns as he could muster, within the walls of the fortress. Hungry and cold, the Jacobites did not make themselves popular. Craig Mair reports in *Stirling: The Royal Burgh*, that 'Military Law was imposed by truck of drum through the town – anyone found near the Castle, or harbouring garrison wives or children, would be shot.' Many local buildings, the Settle Inn included, still bear the marks of musket-fire from the intermittent exchanges which occurred throughout the siege.

A fan, depicting the blood and thunder of the rebel's siege of Stirling, c. 1745. (Picture reproduced by kind permission of the Smith Art Gallery & Museum)

The psychic also reported that a number of the ghostly troops appeared to be speaking French. Again this is a possibility, as a contingent of French soldiers was in the service of the Young Pretender, many under the command of Mirabel de Gordon – a favourite of the prince, and the buffoon who positioned the battery on 'The Gownie': so close to the castle, as the chiding Chevalier Johnstone put it, that 'the enemy could see even the buckles of the shoes of our artillerymen.' The guns were obliterated and Mirabel – known by his ironically-minded critics as 'Mr Admirable' – departed with the rest of Bonnie Charlie's cohort on 1 February, the siege abandoned as the vengeful army of Prince William, 'Bloody Cumberland', approached to relieve the Redcoat garrison. For soldiers and citizens alike this would have been a time of great anxiety, and it is difficult to imagine that the rebels could have resisted the temptation of setting themselves up within an obligingly located ale-house, or that their stresses could not have impressed themselves on this place.

Michael was aware of a strong smell of urine and of 'unkempt people'. The wide streets and prettily gardened council houses of the modern Wynd give every impression of cosy comfort and respectability, but this psychic impression, too, was definitely a historical possibility. Sanitation in the Wynd, home until the 1930s of many densely-packed workmen's lodging-houses, was notoriously bad. 'Noble Dan' Bickerstaffe, mentioned earlier with regard to the 1925 murder of Nessie Reid, rented 'Bed #70' (of 120) in one such dive, not a stone's throw from the inn's entrance. The stench of nitrogen-rich hops from the malt houses and ale & porter breweries which cluttered Irvine Place through much of the nineteenth and early twentieth centuries, might also have given the whole area an odour not entirely unlike that described by the psychic. As the nearest tavern to both the lodgings and the breweries, the Red Lion would have enjoyed the patronage of a great many 'unkempt people'.

Current landlord Declan Dufficy, while wary of Spiritfinders' methodology – though their vigil at the Settle Inn was before his tenancy, he has encountered the group elsewhere – is far from sceptical. The amiable Irishman has no doubt that the place is haunted, but this gives him no cause for concern. 'Why would it?' After many years in the bar business, he says, 'You can tell in some old places that there's something still there. But there's nothing bad here. Nothing at all.' No evidence of the ghost-children's angry parent? 'No. There's an old fella sits by the side of the fireplace facing the bar, and an old girl sits on the other. Sometimes you see them out of the corner of your eye.' He smiles. 'They're quiet. You know? When I'm working here by myself they make good company.'

How far the haunted reputations of many pubs are self-perpetuating is anyone's guess. Old pubs, like castles, are amongst those locations that we *expect* to be occupied by spirits – they are the most conspicuous and accessible symbols of our history and heritage, after all. In *The English Pub*, Michael Jackson and Frank Smyth carried out a survey amongst the country's largest breweries as to how many of their hostelries claimed a resident ghost: 'about one in five' said one; 'too numerous to mention', said another. Were they concerned by the reputation and attention attracted by such tales? Not for a moment: ghosts – as the example of Stirling's two oldest hostelries shows – are *very* good for business.

Swan Song

Les Cygnes, the Thistles Shopping Centre

A bright, friendly, continental coffee shop located in a bustling modern shopping centre would seem an unlikely place to find a ghost. The strip-lit splendour of twenty-first-century consumer culture certainly lacks the grime and gothic glour of many of the Burgh's historic haunted places. Staff at Les Cygnes, occupying Unit 3 of the Thistles Shopping Centre, might be inclined to disagree. A welcoming modern restaurant, boasting 'the best coffee in Scotland', workers here have experienced all manner of curious happenings. I was contacted by staff shortly after the shop opened at the start of the new century. Knowing of my involvement with the Stirling GhostWalk, they wondered if my knowledge of Stirling's supernatural lore might offer some explanation for the soft child-like chuckling unnervingly heard within their toilets, the mischievous misplacing of keys, cups and condiments – which would vanish for days only to reappear, inexplicably, in the most *obvious* locations – and the uneven footfalls which seemed to follow workers as they descended the stairs to the loading bay and store-rooms on the level below.

Assistants at neighbouring Holland & Barrett, I was told at the time, refused to use one area of this level because of its unpleasant atmosphere. Current staff at the health-food shop are unaware of any such reputation, and report none of the strange sensations and events which persist to the present day within the coffee shop. Waitresses often report hearing their names being spoken, only to find no-one nearby. Fleeting shadows are

Les Cygnes – another haunted coffee shop.
(David Kinnaird)

spotted out of the corner of the eye. One young woman sought new employment shortly after taps suddenly spurted full-force behind her in a lower-level washroom. 'She was up those stairs and out of here like a shot,' says the current manager, Enrico Rizza. Enrico's stance on the subject of spirits is less sceptical than it once was. His view changed shortly after the death of his father, when he believed he saw the old man reflected 'almost like a negative image' in a mirror. A sensible chap with little time for talk of the supernatural, he initially thought that his imagination had deceived him – easily done amid the emotional tumult of bereavement – until other family members confirmed identical experiences. Largely unfazed by the prospect of working amongst spirits ('If they're there, they're there – I just get on with things'), he reports feeling just a *little* discomfort when, locking-up the business after late-opening, he is occasionally aware of an oppressive presence. 'It feels like there's someone almost physically pushing me out of the door,' he says, 'like they didn't want me here.'

Kasia Gladun, who has worked at the coffee shop for more than two years, has shared that unsettling sensation, and is as stoical as her employer: resisting the unwelcoming essence's urgings with a simple, 'I'm sorry, but I have to stay.' Kasia reports a number of encounters. Climbing the steps from the lower level, she heard limping footfalls approach her from the direction of the kitchens, passing coldly through her on the stairs. She feels sure that more than one ghost haunts the place. The presence on the stairwell is male, she thinks, and younger than the stern female spirit eager to hasten staff's departure at the end of the working day. She admits that this is an instinctive response, as no visual manifestation has ever occurred: 'They just feel very different.' Kasia admits that she is perhaps more aware of these spirits because she comes from a Polish culture, open to and accepting of the *possibility* of their presence. Like Enrico, her attitude is informed in part by family experience. 'My grandmother died when I was very small – just one month old. I did not know her at all, but I feel she is very close to me, protecting me.' Lodging in rooms next door to Nicky-Tam's, in Baker Street, she feels that she may have also have encountered a ghost there. This, thankfully, is not one of the troublesome occupants of the 'most haunted pub in Scotland', but a more gentle spirit – offering her comfort during homesick hours. A reassuring thought.

The recent historic record offers little obvious explanation for events at Les Cygnes. If construction or redevelopment had prompted activity – as seems to be the case with many modern hauntings – then one might expect the staff of earlier shops which have occupied this unit to have reported similar experiences, but this is not the case. From 1865 until the opening of the Thistles in the late 1970s, much of the Port Street site was occupied by the Stirling Carriage Works of William Kinross & Sons, coach-makers to Queen Victoria – still proudly announcing themselves as 'Carriage and Motor Car builders to the Nobility and Gentry of Great Britain, His Highness the Rajah of Jowar and many other Native Gentlemen of India' well into the twentieth century. The 1858 Ordnance Survey map shows the site of the current coffee house as a pend granting access to the smaller of the Boiler and Dye Houses of the busy Port Mill.

Industry – particularly on the small-scale Stirling model – was largely unregulated during this era. Machinery in woollen mills was not 'boxed' (safely covered) and illness and injury were commonplace – an explanation for the stairwell ghost's peculiar gait, perhaps – but rarely reported. Prior to the 1835 Factory Act, regulating the employment of children, half the workers in Stirling's woollen mills were between eight and fifteen years of age, working from 6 a.m. to 8 p.m. Craig Mair, in *Stirling: The Royal Burgh*, reports the experience of Jane Reid, a small child employed at Smith's Woollen Mill in nearby Cowane Street, who told a government inspector in 1833 that she could expect 'a skelp or so on the lug to keep me at work.' Exhaustion and abuse – and all for the princely sum of 2s 9d a week. While it would be nice to think that the reported childish chuckling and concealment of objects were the japes of wee Jane or her ilk, letting off a little steam after a tortuous day's toil, the reality of their lives would rarely be so jolly.

Two doors along from the restaurant lies another possible source of spectral turmoil. Here can be found a spiral staircase, leading down from the bustle of the shopping centre into another world entirely. Uncovered during the Thistles' construction, this is the Bastion, all that remains of one of the circular corner-towers of the ancient Burgh Wall: a guard room, complete with Bottle Dungeon – or 'Thieves' Pot' – into which drunkards, burglars and other mischief-makers caught by the night-watch could be cast until the Tolbooth opened its doors with the coming dawn. Most likely this was part of Mary de Guise's sixteenth-century fortification of the Burgh's defences, though it could be considerably older.

The Bastion has become a popular (and unexpected) feature for modern shoppers, displaying a little of the town's dark history through decals and dioramas – and featuring the garish figure of 'Justice' which once decorated the town's courtroom. Interestingly, a modern fire door allows access from the Bastion onto the level below the shops, where activity is most frequently reported. Could the ghostly presences within Les Cygnes have some connection with past crimes and misdemeanours? This, certainly, was the theory of one medium who dramatically sought to expel a supposedly penitential phantom here, in 2006. Staff present at the time were singularly unimpressed by this exercise in exorcism – largely because it clearly didn't work.

The doorway leading from the Bastion to the service level beneath Les Cygnes, where staff have had curious experiences. (Patricia Brannigan)

The Thieves' Pot – a dismal Bottle Dungeon beneath the Bastion. (Patricia Brannigan)

The Bastion – a dungeon beneath the modern Thistles shopping centre. The statue of Justice standing vigil in the corner once adorned the Tolbooth court. (Patricia Brannigan)

Contacting Thistles Marketing Manager, Geraldine El Masrour, to arrange to photograph the Bastion for this book, I was told that reports of strange activity were not limited to this small section of the centre. Security guards on the night-watch often reported seeing a female figure out of the corner of their eyes in the Thistle Marches, a 1997 addition to the shops, though none have any ideas as to her identity or purpose – and all are quick to note that the cathedral-like interior of the high-walled, glass-roofed modern mall can play tricks on the eye, and the imagination, in the darkness of night. One guard had a more chilling encounter. As he patrolled the Marches, the lonely click of his heels echoing around him, he stopped, the hairs standing on the back of his neck, sure that someone was lurking close behind him. He turned sharply, and – with a mixture of relief and consternation – found he was alone. Suddenly he felt an unseen force push him hard against the wall, as though strong hands were holding him. After a few moments of panicked, silent struggle, he slumped forward – released by his unseen attacker – and, shaken, he hastened to the security office in the management suite. An experienced professional, and fully aware that telling others of this terrifying encounter might well earn him the mockery of his peers, he chose, nonetheless, to make a formal report of the incident. A source for this encounter is difficult to pinpoint. The Marches are located, like much of the centre, over the site of the expansive Victorian Port Mill, grasslands which once bustled with the activity of the

The Thistle Marches – a security guard claimed to have been attacked here by an 'unseen force'. (David Kinnaird)

port and warehouses which give Port Street its name, and, more recently, a public highway. It remains a mystery, and one – thankfully – which has never been repeated.

Afterword

As I worked on this slim 'volume of forgotten lore', the daughter of friends died, just a few days short of her sixteenth birthday. Eilidh Brown was an astonishing young lady. Over the past year cancer had cost her countless hours of suffering, but for all the pain and woe life slung at her, she fought on. When her lifespan was calculated in days, she wrestled them into months. When the comforting oblivion of unconsciousness beckoned, she dug in her heels, determined not to 'go easy into that good night'. She was a frightened little girl, but remained positive, giving her family and friends faith in the possibility of hope, and the strength to face her ultimate fate. In so doing she was, and remains, inspirational.

Writing of the death, doom and disaster which provide the backdrop of many of the tales in the preceding pages, it is easy to forget that at least some of the stories behind these legends relate to real people, and real tragedies. With some of them – historical and legendary – it is the exceptional circumstances of their passing which has impressed them, forever, on the consciousness of the community.

In Eilidh's case it was, and will continue to be, her example. Her legacy will endure. In her last days she helped establish a Trust to help children like her, seeking treatments and trials often too expensive or experimental to be attainable by ordinary families.

Do I believe in ghosts? I don't think so. No. Do I believe that the spirit of an individual can endure, that the ideas and examples they represented live on? Oh yes. I didn't know her well, but I had hoped to give Eilidh a copy of this book. I shall have to content myself with a dedication and a recommendation to you all: visit the Eilidh Brown Trust: www.eilidhbrown.co.uk

> Death be not proud, though some have called thee
> Mighty and dreadfull, for, thou art not so,
> For, those, whom thou think'st, thou dost overthrow,
> Die not, poore Death, nor yet canst thou kill me.
>
> John Donne

Bibliography

Cook, W.B., 'Notes for a New History of Stirling' (Transactions of the Stirling Natural History Society, Stirling, 1898–1899)

Coventry, Martin, *Haunted Castles & Houses of Scotland* (Goblinshead, Musselburgh, 2004)

Creighton-Smith, Sir James, *Victorian Jottings* (1826), quoted in the *Stirling Sentinel* (21 December 1926)

Drysdale, William, *Old Faces, Old Places and Old Stories of Stirling* (Eneas MacKay, 1898)

Fleming, J.S., *The Old Ludgings of Stirling* (Eneas MacKay, Stirling, 1897)

Fleming, J.S., *Old Nooks of Stirling* (Eneas MacKay, Stirling, 1898)

Fraser, Antonia, *Mary Queen of Scots* (Weidenfelt & Nicolson, London, 1969)

Harrison, John G., 'The World of John Cowane' (a report for Stirling District Council, 1989)

Hippisley Coxe, Antony D. *Haunted Britain* (Book Club Associates, London, 1975):

Holder, Geoff, *The Guide to Mysterious Stirlingshire* (The History Press, 2008)

Jackson, Michael & Smyth, Frank, *The English Pub* (Collins, London, 1976)

Keay, John & Julia, *Collins Encyclopaedia of Scotland* 2nd Edn. (Collins, London, 2000)

Lindsay, Robert, *Historie and Chronicles of Scotland: 1436–1565* (Anaeus MacKay for the Scottish Text Society, 1899)

Mair, Craig, *Stirling: The Royal Burgh* (John Donald, Edinburgh, 1990)

Mair, Craig, 'Alan Mair: Last Man Hanged in Stirling' (Stirling District Libraries, 1993)

Martine, Roddy, *Supernatural Scotland* (Robert Hale, 2003)

McGrail, Steve, 'Spectral Snapshots' *Fortean Times* #92 (November 1996)

Milligan, Christine, 'The Church of the Holy Rude, Stirling: Interpreting the Story' (Come & See Scotland's Churches, 1993)

O'Donnell, Elliott, *Scottish Ghost Stories* (Kegan Paul, Trench, Trubner & Co, London, 1911)

Reilly, Alfred G., 'A Newspaperman Looks Back: Stories of 25 Years', *Stirling Sentinel* (1948)

Ritchie, R.L., 'A Chiel Haes Mind' (Manuscript, 1991)

Robertson, James, *Scottish Ghost Stories* (Warner Books, London, 1996)

Ronald, James, *Landmarks of Old Stirling* (Eneas MacKay, Stirling, 1899)

Small, John W., *The Ludgings of the Earl of Mar* (Eneas MacKay, Stirling, 1905)

Thiselton Dyer, T.F., *Strange Pages from Family Papers* (Low, London, 1895)

Young, Alex F., *Encyclopaedia of Scottish Executions: 1750-1963* (Eric Dobby Publishing, Kent, 1998)

Broadsides for the executions of John Campbell, Alan Mair, John Baird and Andrew Hardie (National Library of Scotland)

The Boys Scrap Book (American Sunday School Union, Philadelphia, 1839)

The Penny Magazine #49 (Charles Knight, London, 5 January 1833)

Other titles published by The History Press

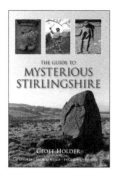

The Guide to Mysterious Stirlingshire

GEOFF HOLDER

This book offers an insight into the mysterious Scottish county of Stirlingshire, detailing the strange and uncanny in an accessible and enchanting way. Every historic site and ancient monument is explored, along with the many hidden treasures to be found in the area. Ruins, tombstones, sculptures and archaeological curiosities are complemented by 100 photographs, making this an indispensable companion for everyone about to journey into the mysterious realms of Stirlingshire.

978 0 7524 4768 1

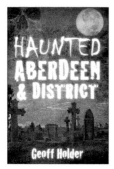

Haunted Aberdeen & District

GEOFF HOLDER

This spine-tingling volume includes Fyvie Castle, home to the Green Lady; Aberdeen Central Library, where the ghost of a former librarian still helps customers; the Four Mile Inn, whose staff have heard ghostly footsteps; and His Majesty's Theatre, said to be haunted by a ghost named Jake. Richly illustrated with over seventy-five photographs and ephemera, this book is sure to appeal to all those interested in finding out more about Aberdeen's haunted heritage.

978 0 7524 5533 4

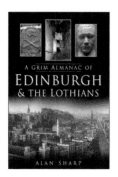

A Grim Almanac of Edinburgh & the Lothians

ALAN SHARP

Beneath the surface respectability of the jewel in the Scottish crown lies a warren of filth-ridden alleys and stairs where thieves, murderers and ghouls of every description planned and carried out their foul deeds. Meet Major Weir, the devil-worshipping black magician and his wicked sister Grizel; Jessie King, the notorious Stockbridge baby farmer; and of course, worst of all, Mr Burke and Mr Hare, who plied their swift trade in corpses for the dissection table of Dr Knox.

978 0 7509 5105 0

Scottish Bodysnatchers: A Gazetteer

GEOFF HOLDER

From burial grounds in the heart of Glasgow to quiet country graveyards in Aberdeenshire, this book takes you to every cemetery ever raided, and reveals where you can find extant pieces of anti-resurrectionist graveyard furniture, from mortsafes, coffin cages and underground vaults to watchtowers and morthouses. Filled with stories of 'reanimated' corpses, daring thefts, black-hearted murders and children sold to the slaughter by their own mothers, this macabre guide will delight residents and visitors alike.

978 0 7524 5603 4

Visit our website and discover thousands of other History Press books.
www.thehistorypress.co.uk